Badass

BONUS MOMS

Strength, Love and the Power of Showing Up

Badass BONUS MOMS

STEPHANIE BAILEY

Miss-Adventures

This book is lovingly dedicated to my two bonus sons, Bruno and Rocco Miller, who inspired me to write it. You are truly the greatest gifts I've been blessed with. Your joy, resilience, and spirits fill my heart with so much love. Thank you for allowing me to be part of your lives, for teaching me the true meaning of love and family, and for letting me be your bonus mom.

I love you both so much!

Every journey into motherhood is unique, and becoming a bonus mom brings its own unimaginable transformations. Imagine stepping into a world where love and loyalty intertwine, where navigating new roles feels like walking a tightrope. This extraordinary adventure is filled with challenges, triumphs, heartwarming moments, and unexpected lessons. Amidst this beautiful chaos, remember that your strength, love, and commitment to showing up make all the difference. Embrace your inner superhero; you have the power to become the Badass Bonus Mom you aspire to be!

"Never do for a child what he can do for himself (
or herself). A "dependent" child is a demanding child…
Children become irresponsible only when we fail to
give them opportunity to take on responsibility."

—Rudolf Dreikurs & Margaret Goldman

Dedications

I dedicate this book to all the incredible women who have embraced the role of parenting their significant other's children. Your courage to step into this journey with love and genuine care—despite the absence of a clear roadmap—is both selfless and profoundly inspiring. You embody resilience, compassion, and the true spirit of family.

To my partner, Damon Miller: thank you for welcoming me into your world and for bringing your wonderful boys into my life. Your unwavering trust and love have opened my heart to new experiences and joys I never imagined possible. Together, we navigate this beautiful adventure of our unique family, and I cherish every moment we share, learning and growing alongside each other.

Lastly, I dedicate this work to God, who continually guides me on every path I take, showering me with unconditional love, grace, and strength. Your presence is my foundation, reminding me of the beauty in this journey.

Ladies, being a Badass Bonus Mom means embracing the beautiful, rewarding challenge of blending families. It involves living with and supporting your partner's children—typically those under eighteen—who need additional guidance. As a bonus mom, you often step into a significant parenting role, navigating the complexities of relationships and responsibilities with love and resilience.

This journey isn't just about managing daily chaos; it's about maintaining your sanity and nurturing your spirit, especially when the path gets tough. It requires courage, patience, and a fierce commitment to positively impacting these children's lives.

Being a Badass Bonus Mom is a rewarding role that transforms both you and the unique family you're building together. Remember, this isn't just a job; it's an adventure that calls for strength and authenticity.

So, how will you embrace this journey with pride?

Disclaimer

Hey, Badass Ladies! Welcome to *Badass Bonus Moms: Strength, Love, and the Power of Showing Up*. This book is a delightful mix of my own wild ride and a few shared escapades of other incredible bonus moms I know. My aim is to be insightful, educational, and immensely supportive—because let's be honest, navigating this journey can feel like herding cats sometimes—all while keeping you entertained.

I wrote this book for anyone currently sailing the uncharted waters of parenting a significant other's kid(s), those pondering if the bonus mom life is their calling, or anyone who loves a bonus mom. My goal is not to offend, embarrass, or insult anyone (unless you're the one whose kid just threw a tantrum in the grocery store—then we're totally in this together!).

The stories and insights I share aren't set in stone—because let's face it, every child and parenting style is as unique as a snowflake. *Badass Bonus Moms* is not a one-size-fits-all manual; every kid comes with their own charming quirks and challenges. So, trust your instincts and intuition; they're your best allies on this unpredictable ride.

May this book bring you laughter, insight, and a sense of camaraderie as we unite as Badass Bonus Moms everywhere. Each chapter is crafted to help you grow wiser, stronger, and more aware of just how bad-ass you truly are for taking on this wild adventure. And remember, you're not alone on this rollercoaster of emotions that sometimes feels like an amusement park ride that just won't end!

Just a friendly reminder: this book is not a substitute for professional therapy, psychiatric advice, or any licensed professional's counsel.

So, grab your favorite drink, a pen, and a journal, and let's dive into your Badass Bonus Moms journey together!

Xoxo,

Stephanie

Contents

Strength, Love, and the Power of Showing Up

Being a Badass Bonus Mom is like being a superhero without a cape—plenty of coffee, a dash of chaos, and a sprinkle of recognition. But the emotional rewards? Those are priceless.

"You're not my mother!" These magical words hit me as I was leaving Bruno's room, and I instinctively stepped back inside. I had braced myself for those words, knowing I was just his dad's girlfriend, but hearing them still stung. I had invested so much time and energy into guiding him, and that statement burned deeper than I expected. Of course, he was right. But my reaction—taking a deep breath, finding my composure, and leading with immense love—what I like to call *The Switzerland Strategy* (a way to remain neutral and supportive)—changed our relationship and set the stage for the incredible bonus-mom journey I'm on.

Stepping into the role of a bonus mom can feel like a superhero transformation. One moment you're enjoying carefree date nights, and the next, you're embracing a new identity faster than Wonder Woman can spin her lasso. You dive into this adventure without a clear job description, greeted by a whirlwind of emotions and the stress of navigating relationships with kids you barely know.

And let's be honest: bonus moms often receive little recognition for their extra work. I vividly remember when Damon's oldest son moved in full-time; it was a thrilling whirlwind. We transitioned from my cozy one-bedroom condo shared by two to a bustling family unit, with his younger son, Rocco, joining us on weekends and every other week during the summer. We hadn't discussed our living situation or parenting styles in-depth—because that's what stepmoms do—and while it was fun at first, reality hit hard. I found myself shouldering a significant amount of the parenting responsibilities. It didn't happen all at once but felt like following breadcrumbs to a feast; I eagerly took the bait. Bedtimes, homework, sibling conflicts, accountability, emotional support, and being the DHO (Disciplinary Hearing Officer)—all the things that came with the territory but were never explicitly discussed—fell on my shoulders. Fun!

Let's face it: being a bonus mom isn't a walk in the park. Say goodbye to solo brunches with friends or squeezing in workouts as often as you used to, but don't worry; you will learn how to balance, because *You Can't Pour From An Empty Cup*— a chapter in this book.

Navigating the complexities of balancing your relationship with your partner while stepping into a parenting role that lacks a clear title—wife, fiancée, stepmother, or pre-biological bond— can be challenging. Parenting your partner's kids can feel like jumping out of a plane without a parachute—exhilarating at first, until reality sets in. Have you ever poured your heart into a job, striving to prove your worth, only to feel unseen, receiving scant reassurance or thank-yous, and feeling like you have to ask for them, just unspoken expectations? That's why I wrote this book.

I see you, and I understand the sacrifices you've made to open your heart to children who aren't your own while supporting a partner you aren't married to. Your efforts deserve recognition and appreciation. I recognize the hard work you've put in and the challenges you continue to face.

Being a Badass Bonus Mom isn't just a new executive title; it's a commitment filled with laughter, exhaustion, the occasional *F-bomb*—another chapter—and a whole lot of life-changing love. You're nurturing kids who aren't yours while navigating dynamics with their mother, who may not always be your biggest fan or acknowledge you. Let's be clear: you're not expected to be Mary Poppins or the perfect parent. Mistakes are part of this journey, and striving for perfection will only wear you out. Embrace the chaos, give yourself grace, and remember that you're a badass for stepping into this new family dynamic.

Your bonus mom journey may be challenging, but it's also incredibly rewarding! It's filled with memories, unconditional love, and the chance to positively influence a child's life. The bonding moments you create—like Bruno calling me "Michelle" and Damon calling me "Princess"—the laughter, the celebrations, the memories, and new traditions are worth all the sweat, tears, stress, and worry. Life is a gamble, and trusting the process is part of the reward.

So take a deep breath, give yourself a high-five, and know you're not alone. You've found the perfect guide to help you navigate the wild ride of being a Badass Bonus Mom. Join me as I share stories from my journey, along with heartfelt quotes taken from cards and messages (in no particular order) that Bruno, Rocco, and Damon gave and sent me that remind me—even on the toughest days—that my efforts haven't gone unnoticed. The love we've built is one of the greatest gifts I've been blessed with.

The insights I share may resonate, and if not, that's okay. My goal is for you to know you are not alone on this journey you are choosing or are already on. The strength, love, and power of showing up is an extraordinary gift. May you learn something new, laugh freely, feel understood and validated, and discover joy in the smallest moments.

Grab your favorite drink, settle in, and let's embark on this Badass Bonus Moms journey together!

Xoxo,
Stephanie (One Badass Bonus Mom to another)

Journal Prompt:

What Do You Value in Your Partner's Child(ren)?

Take a moment to list the names of the children in your life and the qualities you admire and love about them. Life can get busy, but carving out a few minutes for this practice—whether daily or weekly—can truly enrich your experience as a bonus mom.

Embrace this ritual as a way to empower yourself on your journey. **Remember, this is a celebration of the unique individuals in your life.** Reflect on the moments that make you smile, the quirks that endear them to you, and the strengths that impress you.

Try to jot down specific examples or fond memories that highlight these qualities. Keep this list accessible, and whenever feelings of frustration arise, review it to remind yourself why you chose to embrace this role. Let it serve as a source of inspiration and a reminder of your motivation.

Happy Bonus-Mom Day Stephanie!

So grateful for all you do for me in helping shape me into the best version of myself. You have helped me go down the right path and made my life so much less stressful. I don't know where I would be without you, and I hope you know how grateful I am to have you in my life. Thank you for always being there for me and for being someone I can always talk to and rely on.
Love you, and thanks for everything.

Love, Bruno

What a Badass Bonus Mom Is

You've already glimpsed what it means to be a Badass Bonus Mom, but it's essential to recognize just how incredible you are and why. So, let's explore this role further. A Badass Bonus Mom is an empowering, motherly figure who plays a vital role in parenting her partner's child or children—those for whom he has full-time or shared custody—while living under the same roof. She embraces the challenge of nurturing, guiding, and supporting these children, often stepping into a primary parenting role.

This is not a passive position; you're not a bystander in the household. You're actively invested in their growth, well-being, and future. In this dynamic, a Badass Bonus Mom establishes essential boundaries, fosters open communication, and promotes accountability. She creates a supportive environment where basic respect is non-negotiable, ensuring everyone understands that disrespect simply isn't an option. Her main goal is to create genuine harmony—as much as possible—in a blended household while managing the sometimes chaotic nature of family life. This means setting limits, speaking your truth—even when it's uncomfortable—and remaining steady and patient as bonds develop. Remember, boundaries aren't walls; they're the foundation of a healthy, functioning family.

While navigating this new family structure, a Badass Bonus Mom prioritizes her relationship with her partner—to whom she is not engaged or married—ensuring that love and understanding flourish between them. This connection is critical because your romantic relationship is the anchor of the entire household. When you and your partner are aligned and communicating effectively, everything else tends to fall into place. The children sense the stability that comes from a solid partnership. And let's be real: sometimes, a little intimacy can calm your inner Tasmanian devil!

At the same time, she learns to love and care for her partner's children as if they were her own, all while balancing work and a social life. This is the beautiful, yet delicate, dance of being a Badass Bonus Mom. It's not about abandoning yourself or your needs; it's about expanding your capacity to love and nurture while maintaining your identity, dreams, and well-being. You model what it looks like to be a complete person who shows up fully for those you love.

Though it's not always easy, this book will guide you as you navigate this journey. Being a Badass Bonus Mom isn't just about parenting; it's about building genuine connections, embracing challenges with courage, and celebrating the joys of blending families. It's recognizing that you didn't have to take this path—you chose to. And that choice matters every single day, especially on the tough ones. This journey requires strength, patience, and a whole lot of heart. It asks you to show up even when you're exhausted, to forgive yourself when you lose your patience (which will happen), and to keep caring and loving even when that love isn't immediately returned or recognized. Most importantly, it requires you to believe that you matter—because you absolutely do. Ladies, give yourselves a well-deserved pat on the back because you are truly amazing. You're not just an additional figure in these kids' lives; you're a force for good, a source of stability, a woman brave enough to love fiercely, even when there's no guarantee that love will be understood or appreciated. That's not just good parenting—that's Badass. Now, let's dive in.

The Initial Introduction

Meeting your partner's family or friends can be nerve-wracking, but nothing compares to meeting his children. Damon and I had been together for a year and three months. He'd shared photos and videos of his boys for months, but nothing—absolutely nothing—prepared me for meeting them in person. When you envision a future with someone, meeting their kids feels monumental. I knew it mattered to Damon, which meant it mattered to me. Unfortunately, my body staged a full-blown panic attack. Yikes!

My palms, forehead, and upper lip were sweating as if I'd just completed a marathon, and my entire body quivered as my heart raced. I couldn't stop staring at the clock in my friend Deb's kitchen. Deb and her husband, Jules, were hosting a casual football gathering—a perfect opportunity, we all thought. The laid-back setting included kids and another family. Damon could introduce his two boys, Rocco and Bruno, as "friends" instead of announcing that we lived together. Plus, Damon's boys loved football, and Deb's sons were the same age. It seemed ideal. What I didn't anticipate was the flood of sweat and my lack of control. I glanced at the clock again. Seriously?! I'd taught yoga classes with over sixty people, cool as a cucumber, but this? I felt like I was about to spontaneously combust. "Here's a pepper; chop it for the salad to distract you," Deb said, reading me like a book. She reassured me that Damon's sons would love me. I took multiple deep breaths, trying to calm my nerves, and focused on chopping. Then they walked into the kitchen.

I froze and began chopping faster, praying I wouldn't slice off a finger. My mind blank, I struggled to think of what to say. Damon introduced Deb first, then turned to me. My voice, normally steady, came out in a shrill squeak. "Hi, so nice to meet you both!" Their eyes widened and darted to their dad before they asked where Deb's sons were. Thankfully, Deb jumped in with an answer, and as the boys left the kitchen, I could finally breathe; I'd been holding my breath for what felt like hours. I was on high alert the rest of the day. Every time Damon's boys entered a room, my antennae went up. I was hyperaware of how close we were sitting, whether they noticed me, and what they were thinking. I checked on them constantly, asking if they needed anything, offering to fill their plates, and getting them drinks. I smothered them with kindness, hoping they'd think I was amazing. By the end of the night, a wave of relief washed over me. I did it! I met his sons and showered them with kindness. How could they not like me? Famous last words.

As we were leaving, Damon casually mentioned, "I need to give Stephanie a ride home on the way to dropping you guys off at your mom's." "Thanks, bae," slipped out of my mouth like a toddler who'd just learned to say "mama" for the first time. Oh. My. God. Bruno and Rocco's heads snapped up like meerkats, their eyes wide. They exchanged glances, clearly processing what they'd just heard. In that split second, I remembered: they didn't know we were living together. They had no clue about the "bae" situation. My pupils expanded to the size of dinner plates—and I have large pupils. Think fast! "Thanks, bae," I quickly repeated, gesturing vaguely at Deb. "I mean, thanks to all of you—bae, bae, bae—I call everyone bae. It's just a thing I do." I threw "bae" around like confetti, trying to blur the trail. Their confusion didn't disappear, but at least I planted some doubt. Awkward doesn't even begin to describe that moment.

Less than a week later, Damon finally told his sons about me and our relationship. Surprisingly, the conversation went much better than he had anticipated. Bruno even said, "Yeah, I thought she was your girlfriend." A few weeks after that, they came over to my condo to help their dad and grandfather assemble a dresser. It was another slightly awkward moment of getting to know each other, but this time with a lot less pressure.

Then came Thanksgiving dinner with Damon, Damon's mom, Bruno, and Rocco—the pivotal moment that would shift everything. After dinner, while I was in the basement taking linens to the laundry room, Bruno came downstairs, looked at me with those big brown eyes, and asked, "Can I move in with you and Dad?" He explained that he didn't want to move to the mountains with his mom because all his friends lived in Denver, and his reasoning was sound. When I asked if he'd be okay not seeing his younger brother Rocco full-time, he immediately said yes. Those big brown eyes, that radiating eagerness—I could barely resist. But I also knew this was no casual question; this was a big deal. I reminded him how small my condo was, that he'd be sleeping on the couch. "I don't care!" he exclaimed, his determination shining bright. I looked at him and said, "Okay. Let's clear this with your dad, and if he's okay with it—and your mom agrees—then I'm fine with you living with us." And that's how it happened: not with a grand family meeting or strategic planning session, but with a kid during Thanksgiving asking if he could move in, and me saying yes.

What I didn't know at that moment was that this decision was going to change everything. Blending families isn't just about sharing space; it's about navigating completely new territory. It's about learning to live with people you barely know, figuring out routines you've never had before, and discovering that you're capable of far more than you thought. It's messy, chaotic, and beautiful all at once, and it can change your life overnight.

The Reality of Overnight Change

*Stephanie, your co-parenting in our house
makes all of us enriched with love. Love, Damon.*

Change isn't always terrifying, but it becomes so when a fantasy turns into a nightmare. Mine started one Tuesday at 8 AM. I was standing in the kitchen of my one-bedroom condo, still half-asleep, when I realized I didn't know the teenage boy eating cereal at my coffee table. Not literally; it was Bruno. But emotionally, I had no framework for him. A year earlier, Damon and I were living in our cozy bubble, just the two of us. I could walk around naked, shower spontaneously, and my bathroom and schedule were mine. Everything was mine—including Damon, in my head. Then Bruno moved in before Christmas, and suddenly, nothing was mine anymore: not the bathroom, not the living room (now his bedroom), not my mornings or evenings, and not even my relationship with Damon, which had completely transformed. I remember thinking during those first few weeks, *"This will settle down in a couple of months. Everyone will adjust. We'll find our rhythm.*" I was spectacularly wrong. Here's what people don't tell you about overnight change: the living situation changes instantly, but everything else takes years. The morning Bruno moved in, my life transformed in about five seconds. I imagined living together would be like a sitcom—some awkward moments, a heartfelt conversation, and then everyone would slot into their roles perfectly. That wasn't the case.

I went from being a woman with agency over her own space to feeling like I was squeezing into a stranger's life. Except he wasn't a stranger; he was my partner's son, and I had zero parenting experience—especially with a teenager. I thought I had time to figure it out. I told myself, "Give it a couple of months, and we'll establish routines. Once they settle in, things will feel normal. The awkwardness is temporary." What I didn't understand was the difference between a living situation changing overnight and actually adjusting to that change. One happens in five seconds; the other takes years. Then there was the intimacy shift...Our passionate, can't-keep-our-hands-off-each-other, eyes-rolling-to-the-back-of-my-brain sex, ladies? I never imagined that would change. Why would I? I wasn't a parent, just a fur-baby parent to my cat, and that never changed anything. However, when Bruno moved in, our sex life took a back seat and shifted dramatically, not because Damon stopped wanting me, but because suddenly, there was a thirteen-year-old sleeping twenty feet away, plus a ten-year-old when Rocco came. Also, a bedroom door with a broken lock—which meant I could never actually relax—and one small bathroom for all of us to share meant no more sexy showers with Damon or naked runs to the bathroom after sex. Great.

The spontaneity Damon and I had developed, along with the

routines that defined our early relationship, just...evaporated. Before Bruno moved in, we could have sex at 2 PM on a Saturday or enjoy intimate nighttime connection gazing into each other's eyes, surrounded by candlelight, music, and a glass of wine—almost every night. Sappy, I know, but I loved it. We could be loud. We could be messy. We could leave the bedroom door open if we wanted and, frankly, have sex wherever we wanted. Now? I was hyperaware—always—of every sound, of every possibility that one of the boys could walk in, or the fact that they were right there, on the other side of the wall. Even though logically they couldn't hear everything—if we were really, r-e-a-l-l-y quiet—I felt like they could, like I was committing some kind of betrayal by having a sexual relationship with their father. It took me thirteen months (yes, I was counting) before I could actually relax enough to enjoy intimacy without feeling like I was doing something wrong.

Thirteen. Months. And Damon didn't understand why. "They're asleep!" he'd say, like an excited teenager whose parents finally fell asleep and he could sneak his girlfriend in the house. Or "They're fine," like these were words of foreplay. But I wasn't fine. No amount of reassurance from him could expedite my nervous system's process of trusting that it was okay to be sexual in a home with teenage boys—boys who weren't mine. This uncharted territory was challenging for us. He wanted things to feel normal—the new normal: less quiet, but only when the boys were asleep or playing outside. I couldn't find normal. He wanted to connect physically—after the boys were asleep. I wanted to wait until the boys were away visiting their mom. Ladies, your partner will likely not understand this timeline. He's been their parent their whole life; for him, having them in the house is normal. For you? It's a complete reorganization of your nervous system, and you can't simply speed it up through will-power alone. Honesty, while still trying to be sexy, is exhausting.

A few weeks after Bruno moved in, I emerged from the bedroom, feeling cute in my Lululemon workout gear, to head to a yoga class with Damon. To my dismay, snack wrappers littered the living room floor (which was now Bruno's bedroom), crumbs covered the coffee table, wet towels were piled on the chair, socks were scattered in front of the TV, and Bruno and Rocco were snoozing away. And my partner stood in the kitchen, calmly making coffee as if this was fine—as if any of this was fine. "How is it possible," I whispered, trying to keep my voice from shaking, "that they don't know to throw garbage away?" "They're just boys," Damon casually whispered back, not even looking at me. Something inside me snapped. "They're your boys. And they live here. How do they not know basic house rules?" "Bae, they'll learn..." "When?" I interrupted. "When exactly? Because right now, I feel like I'm living in a dorm room, not a home." Let's be real: trying to be the "cool" girlfriend while maintaining sex appeal, composure, and not losing your mind is a hard task, to say the least.

He looked at me, genuinely confused, as if I was being unreasonable for wanting basic cleanliness in my own home. This was difficult to reconcile because Damon *is* a clean person. He cleans up after himself, makes the bed, and pitches in with cooking and cleaning, so his casual attitude was baffling. That's when I realized our timelines were completely different. Ugh. Timeline discrepancies...I'd imagined I'd have a few weeks to adjust to this change, but he seemed to think I should already be adjusted. In his mind, this wasn't really a change—it was just his normal life, now with me in it and a home address change. The gap between those two timelines became a chasm.

I hadn't imagined I'd spend just over a year feeling anxious during sex, or that I'd need to have conversations about basic household rules that shouldn't require discussion at all, or that I'd be surprised every month by how much more groceries cost when you're feeding a growing teenage boy and a ten-year-old. I didn't imagine that my partner—whom I love—would defend his kids' right to interrupt us at any moment, that he'd struggle to see my contributions as real work, or that he'd use the phrase "They're just boys" like it explained and excused everything. I thought the hard part would be the first month or so. When I was wrong about that, I thought it would be the first three, four, or maybe five months. Wrong again.

The hard part was the year after, and the year after that. Because overnight change—where you suddenly have people living in your space who aren't yours, who don't know you, who are grieving the loss of their original family unit even if they don't say it—doesn't settle down quickly. It settles down s-l-o-w-l-y, with lots of patience, with conversation, with the willingness to have the same discussion multiple times because your partner didn't hear you the first time, and with the understanding that your timeline isn't his, and neither is wrong—they're just differ-ent. Ladies, the overnight change isn't the living situation itself. It's the fact that your whole life has changed, and your partner doesn't realize it yet because his life hasn't changed *much*—he's just added you to it. The adjustment isn't quick; it's not a few weeks of awkwardness followed by smooth sailing. It's years or more of small conversations, moments of understanding, periods of frustration, and the slow process of your nervous system learning that it's safe to be vulnerable in a home with other people—creating successful change means letting go of expectations. The expectations you have—about how quickly things will settle, how soon the kids will adjust, how soon you'll feel at home again—are probably going to be wrong, not because you're unrealistic, but because nobody actually knows how long this takes until they're living it. Every new bonus mom's family dynamic will be different, with different kids, personalities, situations, parenting styles, or perceived expectations. Overnight change doesn't happen overnight; it's measured in years, not weeks, and that's not a failure—that's just reality. So, if you're in those early months, feeling like things should be settling down but they're not, you're not doing it wrong. You're just in the part where the actual work begins—the part after the big change, when everyone has to figure out who they are in this new configuration. That's not a moment; it's a journey, and it takes longer than you think. Be patient; in the long run, it will be worth it.

The slow shifts that make a difference...

Eventually—and this took a long time—a few things shifted. Damon started noticing, not because I asked him to, but because he had to parent alone for a few months while I was in Texas dealing with health issues or when I was gone visiting my best friend Kimberly in California or my mom in New York for a week or a long weekend. Suddenly, he realized how much work it was, how many decisions you have to make every single day, how exhausting it is to be the only adult in the room. When I came back from any of my trips, Bruno greeted me with so much love and appreciation, making my heart realize that even my "stricter" parenting style was making a difference in his life.

When you stop and let go...

I stopped expecting gratitude. When I gave up the idea that Damon would thank me for buying gifts or planning holidays, or buying groceries and shopping, or taking on the predominant parenting role in our household, the resentment lessened. It's still work, but it's work I'm doing because I choose to, not because I expect recognition. Damon started noticing and saying, "Thank you" more often—music to my ears. Over a six-year span, Damon became more supportive and helpful with his boys as we both learned what building our family dynamic meant. As you navigate your Badass Mom journey, remember that every challenge is an opportunity for growth. You are not just a participant in your partner's life; you are a strong, resilient force shaping a new family dynamic. Embrace the messiness and the chaos, for it's in these moments that you'll discover your own strength and the depth of your love. You're doing the hard work, and it matters. Trust the process, and know that you are creating a uniquely beautiful, unconditionally loving blended family—one day at a time.

Be Messy, Be Real

Happy bonus mom day! Rocco

Life is too short to be anyone but your fabulous self, a truth that can change everything. Trying to be someone you're not to win over your partner's kids is a recipe for disaster. Children are perceptive and can sense inauthenticity immediately. They'll either see through your act and view you as a pushover, or they'll watch your facade crumble, leading to emotional fallout directed at them or your partner. You don't deserve that burden. The best gift you can give yourself and your family is your authentic self. When I first became a bonus mom, I thought I had to be "perfect." I tiptoed around Bruno and Rocco, constantly second-guessing myself and trying to fit into a mold of what a bonus mom should be: kind, giving, fun, and always agreeable.

The pressure felt suffocating. Society paints an unrealistic picture of blended families—flawless relationships and seamless interactions. But perfection is a myth that leaves you feeling inadequate and exhausted. I realized I couldn't hide behind a carefully constructed version of myself any longer and asked myself: what's the point? These boys didn't need perfect; they needed real. They needed to get to know me, and that wasn't going to happen behind a mask. That's when everything shifted. Children crave authenticity. They want to connect with the real you, not a version crafted for approval. The moment I let go of my façade and allowed myself to be vulnerable, the dynamic changed. When I felt overwhelmed or unsure, I said so. "Hey, I'm still learning how to navigate this unique family, and some-times I make mistakes." That honesty fostered trust and opened lines of communication.

Being unapologetically myself had always been my approach to life, so why was I trying to be different for my partner's kids? I was exhausted from trying to maintain a smile that looked more like a grimace than genuine joy. I remember a moment when Damon and I had a disagreement in the car. It escalated, and when we pulled up to my condo, Bruno jumped out and headed inside. Sensing he was upset—our fight had triggered memories of his parents' arguments—I followed him. I could see it in his tears and shaking body. I hugged him and apologized for fight-ing in front of him, reassuring him that our disagreement didn't mean we were breaking up. Bruno feared that if we split, he would have to move away. Hearing that was painful, especially since I had agreed to let him live with us. As I explained that my decision had allowed him to stay in Denver, my emotions bubbled over, and I cried while expressing my commitment. In that moment, Bruno hugged me tightly, and I knew our bond was meant to be.

Bruno wasn't just my bonus son; he was a blessing in my life, bringing lessons that would change me forever. Loving someone means sharing the good, the bad, and the messy parts of who you are. Once I embraced this, Bruno and Rocco had the chance to love me fully, just as I loved them. They could be their authentic selves, too. Authenticity means showing your true emotions. It's easy to wear a brave face, but when you allow yourself to be real—whether joyful or stressed—you forge connections that last. Sharing your feelings models emotional honesty and strengthens your relationships in ways perfection never could. That moment with Bruno, when he recognized my concern for him, laid the foundation for trust. Creating a safe space for him to express his feelings while I shared mine encouraged open dialogue. He learned he could talk to me about anything and that he would be validated and heard.

Here's the truth: trying to be anyone else is exhausting, and it will catch up with you. You'll have freak-out moments, feel overwhelmed, and question your abilities. But that's not a sign you're failing—that's being human. Embracing authenticity doesn't mean you won't struggle; it means acknowledging those feelings and being honest about them. When you show your humanity, it allows the kids to feel safe expressing their emotions, learning that ups and downs are part of family life. Releasing the need for perfection frees you from the burden of maintaining an unattainable standard, allowing you to invest in genuine connections instead of fixating on who you think you should be. Find joy in the little moments—a shared laugh or bonding over a favorite movie. These experiences create lasting memories that form the foundation of your relationship with your bonus kids.

Authenticity builds trust. When your bonus kids see you being real, they're more likely to reciprocate, feeling comfortable expressing themselves without fear of judgment. This creates an environment where everyone feels valued and understood—a beautiful cycle of openness.

Ladies, self-acceptance is powerful. Your story and journey

are worth celebrating. Acknowledge your achievements, big or small, whether navigating a challenging family situation or simply making it through a hectic day. Give yourself credit; you're doing great. Extend grace to yourself; stumbling in uncharted waters is normal. Embrace the learning curve.

When you prioritize authenticity over perfection, the kids respond positively. They'll appreciate your honesty and mirror that behavior in their own lives. Releasing the need for perfection allows you to prioritize your well-being. So, ditch the idea of perfection and focus on being the best version of yourself. Celebrate your quirks, strengths, flaws, and even your freak-out moments. Each of these elements makes you uniquely you, and being authentically you is an act of self-love.

You're Badass Bonus Moms, and your voice, passions, and quirks make you extraordinary. When you show up as your true self, you inspire everyone around you to do the same. Let's commit to being unapologetically ourselves; your authenticity is your superpower. It creates lasting bonds through real, raw moments, not perfect ones. A family environment where everyone feels free to be who they are is a gift that keeps on giving.

What the Search Results Don't Tell You

4 years have flown by. You make every year more special.
You are my Heart & Soul. Love Damon

Many textbook "experts" haven't lived in your shoes, so how can they guide you to success? Expert advice often includes phrases like "give kids time to adjust" and "expect a gradual process." That sounds helpful in theory, but it doesn't prepare you for the reality of how long "gradual" actually is.

Imagine walking into a party where the only person you know is the host. Now, imagine there's no alcohol, everyone speaks a different language, and instead of a party you can leave whenever you want, this has turned into your life. Welcome to being a bonus mom and navigating co-parenting your partner's kids!

Here's the thing: research indicates that children aged 10–14 have the most difficulty adjusting to stepfamilies. However, this research doesn't address how this dynamic relates to a bonus mom who isn't *married* to the child's parent. Children need time to adjust and accept boundaries—boundaries that you, as the bonus mom, will likely be enforcing, even as they resist. Fun! All while your partner watches, possibly uncomfortably, especially if he has passed the parenting baton to you, hoping that you and his children will magically get along. Huh...well, this approach isn't helpful.

Research also suggests making parenting changes before remarrying. But, again, what if the bonus mom isn't married, only living with the child's parent? What if the change wasn't planned, but happened organically, such as when his child asked to move in with big brown eyes, and you agreed without fully processing the decision? Or what if your partner surprises you with the change: "Ta-da! My kid(s) are going to be living with us full-time or part-time. Aren't you excited?"

About three weeks after Bruno moved in, Rocco came for his first overnight visit in this new configuration. We had purchased them a queen-size pullout couch, upgraded to a high-end mattress, and put matching sheets, pillowcases, and a blanket on it—the whole thing. It was in the living room, which meant they went to bed, we went to bed, and everyone was supposed to sleep. Damon tucked them both in, said goodnight, and started heading to our bedroom. Rocco shot up like a jack-in-the-box, jolted by a sudden surge of emotion. "You're not sleeping out here with us?" he asked. Damon laughed as if it was ridiculous. "No, buddy. Where would I sleep?" "Here. Next to me. Or on the floor?" I watched this moment unfold from the bathroom as I brushed my teeth, and I could see Damon doing the math, trying to figure out how to make this work and how to make his son feel secure. "There's no room next to you," Damon said gently. "And I'm definitely not sleeping on the hardwood floor."

Rocco looked genuinely confused; the idea of his dad choosing to sleep in a bed with his girlfriend instead of on the floor next to him just didn't compute. Before he could argue further, Bruno's voice came from the darkness. "Rocco, leave it alone." We could hear them whispering after that—Bruno, the older brother, explaining the situation to his younger brother in words a ten-year-old could understand, an acceptance, a boundary. Rocco finally settled down. As Damon approached, I thought, *This wasn't going to be quick*. These kids weren't going to wake up one morning and simply accept that their dad had a girlfriend, that she lived here, that she was a permanent fixture in their lives. They needed time, and not just a little bit. They needed *their* time, while I waited patiently.

Research talks about "small investments that may one day yield a lot of interest." It's beautiful language, but in real life, it feels less like "investing" and more like throwing money into a void and hoping something grows: your bonus kids' promise of eternal affection and, one day, taking care of you when you're old, or a proposal and marriage from your partner—if that's what you want. That's the difference between research and reality.

Fast-forward, before I knew it, I was buying gifts, ordering birthday cakes, coordinating holidays, doing laundry for two teenage boys, and planning grocery runs for appetites that seemed to grow exponentially every week. In those early years, I did it all without fully knowing if Bruno and Rocco noticed or cared. There weren't consistent thank-yous right away or acknowledgments of the labor. I would make dinner, serve the plates, and wait for a "thank you" that rarely happened, or at least a smile or nod that they liked what they were eating—especially in the first year. While my partner could have reassured me that my efforts were valuable, he was often too preoccupied with being the "fun dad" to offer that confirmation in the moment.

This left me feeling unseen as a bonus mom. Fortunately, this dynamic eventually changed.

Ladies, every small step builds a stronger bridge. Every dinner you make, every birthday cake you order, and every awkward moment you navigate is a testament to your love and commitment. Remember, you're not just stepping into their lives; you're creating a new family dynamic. As you embrace the challenges, know that your efforts are planting seeds for a future where laughter fills the rooms, where love grows stronger, and where everyone learns to appreciate each other in their own way.

The bonus mom road may be bumpy, but each twist and turn is a chance for growth—both for you and for them, and for the new family you are building. You're not just Badass Bonus Moms; you're a vital part of this journey. Your voice matters, your feelings matter, and your presence is a gift that will shape their lives in ways you may not see right away. So hold your head high, embrace the chaos, and trust that this beautiful, messy process is worth every single moment.

The Financial Reckoning

About a year into co-parenting Bruno and Rocco, I reviewed my bank account and was shocked to discover that my grocery bill had tripled. I was also buying gifts for extra birthdays and contributing to holiday celebrations we hadn't planned. Expenses that should have been between Damon and his ex had become my financial responsibility because I was the one at home. I was the one thinking ahead, asking, "Don't we need to get them something for Easter, their birthdays (which are both in June), or Christmas?" I started tracking every gift card, birthday cake, "nice family dinner at home," and every message from Damon that started with, "While you're out, can you grab?" which meant I was buying groceries for three or four people (depending on whether Rocco was staying with us) instead of two. One month, I realized I'd spent almost $700 on things for the boys that Damon hadn't requested or offered to pay for.

As these expenses continued to mount month after month,

year after year, I finally brought it up when my savings started dwindling. "I've been thinking about the financial aspect of this," I said. "What do you mean?" Damon asked. "I mean I'm spending a lot of money on your kids, and I love them, I really do. But I didn't sign up to be their financial provider, and I'm starting to feel resentful." He became defensive. "I provide for them. They're my responsibility." "I know, I wasn't implying you didn't," I said. "But I'm living with them. I'm the one who notices when we need groceries. I'm the one who thinks about their birthdays, Starbucks, lunches, or snacks when I'm running errands with the boys, and I'm paying for it with my own money."

The conversation resolved nothing, only creating awkwardness. Ugh. Years passed before Damon proactively inquired about purchases for the boys, finally understanding the need for financial transparency. Instead of letting anger fester, I chose to agree to disagree. Eventually, I stopped scrutinizing my spending, focusing instead on the joy and security I was helping to build, and learning invaluable lessons. This struggle taught me that open financial conversations are crucial in blended families. Though uncomfortable, they pave the way for understanding and collaboration, and they need to happen immediately, not after investments are made. As a bonus mom, advocating for your needs and setting boundaries is essential and empowering. Remember, you're not just co-parenting; you're building a new family dynamic. It's okay to voice concerns and expectations, creating a partnership based on mutual respect and shared responsibility, ensuring everyone's contributions—financial or otherwise—are recognized and valued. Embrace your strength and lead the way. As you navigate these financial discussions, know that you are not just managing expenses; you are shaping your blended family's future. Each conversation builds a foundation of trust and collaboration. Your voice matters, and your perspective is invaluable in creating a harmonious environment. Hold your head high, embrace these challenges, and remember that every step you take strengthens your family. You're not just a bonus mom; you are a trailblazer, and your courage to speak up will create a brighter, more balanced future for your family.

The Privacy Fiasco

*Merry Christmas—thanks for doing all the little things
for me, things I didn't even think I wanted, love Rocco.*

Life can suddenly resemble an episode of the sitcom, *Three's
Company*. The first time Rocco barged into our bedroom without knocking while I was half-dressed, I was mortified and
screamed. "Shut the door! I'm getting dressed!" became my
new catchphrase. He scattered, mortified, and Damon went
after him, presumably to explain the importance of knocking
before entering someone's bedroom, especially since the lock
was broken. But the damage was done. I now associated my
bedroom with panic instead of safety, which exposed me to a
harsh reality. For months, I got dressed either in the bathroom
or behind the bedroom door, just in case. I showered with the
door locked and the shower curtain completely closed, unable
to relax even though nobody was trying to look at me.

My own home—the space that had been my sanctuary—had
become a place where I felt constantly exposed. Damon didn't
quite understand why I needed him to lock the door, to tell his

kids to knock, to create a boundary that clearly designated, "This is Stephanie's and Dad's private space." It took multiple conversations and many moments of me being upset, but eventually, Damon fixed the lock, and the kids learned to knock. Eventually, my nervous system learned that it was safe to be vulnerable in my own bedroom. But that took time—months and months. Here's what I wish someone had said to me when Bruno moved in: Your living situation will change overnight, and your adjustment will take time. Your nervous system will need time to recalibrate. Your relationship will need time to redefine itself. Your financial situation will need time to be discussed and renegotiated. Your boundaries will need time to be established and reinforced. None of that will happen in a few weeks, a few months, or even a year. It's going to take time—Y-E-A-R-S.

Navigating uncharted waters can be challenging. Typically, married couples figure things out together, and future stepmoms discuss and make parenting agreements before marriage. But what happens when you're not engaged or getting married, and simply living together, figuring it out as you go? What if you're navigating this ship solo because your partner doesn't know how to guide you? Wonderful. But let's be real: you're going to have many painful conversations about things you didn't even know you needed to discuss. You're going to feel blindsided by how much this affects your intimate life, your private space, and your finances. You might spend months thinking, "Why doesn't this feel normal yet?" Because it's not supposed to feel normal yet. You're undergoing a massive life change, and your partner—who's been parenting all along—might not understand why you can't adjust faster.

My partner, Damon, had never been in this situation. He was married and had time to develop his parenting style with his ex since his kids were born. He wasn't equipped to understand parenting dynamics outside of marriage, let alone guide me. And I didn't want him to think I wasn't accepting of him, his boys, or this new journey he wanted to share with me. So, I jumped in without a life jacket, hoping I could figure out how to swim to shore on my own—with a school of piranhas chasing me. Well, the more I practiced, the more confident I became.

Regaining your privacy takes time. As the boys grew older, the privacy issue lessened significantly. The boys knock almost all the time, especially if our door is shut (and we have a working bedroom door lock). Also, with a much bigger space, there's naturally more privacy for all of us now that the boys have their own room with four walls and a door.

Remember, Badass Bonus Moms, Rome wasn't built in a day. Navigating this journey is about growth—for both you and the kids. Each step forward is a victory, and every uncomfortable conversation is a building block for a stronger family dynamic. Embrace the process, trust your instincts, and know that it's okay to take the time you need to feel comfortable in your own home. Celebrate your journey and embrace the growth ahead. As you navigate these challenges, remember that every hurdle you overcome demonstrates your strength and resilience. You're not just adapting; you're thriving in a new environment that requires patience and understanding.

Each awkward moment and every lesson learned is a step toward creating a loving, supportive family. Trust the process and give yourself grace. Reclaiming your space and privacy underscores your commitment to this new life, as you build something beautiful. Keep shining, keep growing, and know that you are making a difference—not just for yourself, but for the blended family you are nurturing every single day.

First Freak-Out

Happy new year love you. Rocco.

Freakouts are inevitable. You might not know when they'll happen, or how, but often the reality is different from what you expect.

I remember when Bruno first moved into my 583-square-foot one-bedroom condominium. It was shortly after COVID hit, and with his classes going virtual, Damon gave me a choice: I could claim the bedroom for eight hours a day, or Bruno could. Either way, I was losing my space. Meanwhile, Damon headed off to his office—the only place still functioning since no other coworkers were there during lockdown. He had his own office, his own meeting room, his own escape. I was stuck in a pressure cooker with a teenager I was still getting to know, unable to go to work, unable to leave, unable to breathe. I had tried to communicate my needs, dropping subtle hints, casually mentioning, "Wouldn't it be fun if Bruno went to your office with you?" hoping Damon would pick up on the subtext. I hinted at feeling trapped. But Damon didn't get it, or maybe he did and just didn't want to deal with it. Either way, my quiet communication wasn't working.

The first few days were fine, but by day three, I was losing my mind. The nagging thought ran on repeat: Why does Damon get to escape to his office while I'm stuck here taking care of his son? I loved my condo, but I hated being confined to it. I couldn't stand the thought of Bruno sprawled on our bed, feet on our pillows, snacking during his virtual classes while I tiptoed around my own home like a visitor in someone else's life. It felt less like parenting and more like punishment—mine. Damon would come home grinning from ear to ear, while I was vibrating with rage. After bottling it up for several days, trying to be the "good bonus mom" who doesn't complain, I had my moment. I yelled. Really yelled. "You need to take your kid to work with you! I'm not going to sit here, tiptoeing around my own fucking house, feeling like a prisoner while you get to enjoy your office space. You have room there—be a parent and take Bruno with you! And I don't give a flying fuck if you don't want to!" Yeah, it was bad. What surprised me was that the next day, Damon took Bruno to his office—not reluctantly, not with an attitude, but as if he finally understood that this wasn't about me being difficult; it was about me drowning. By the time they came home, a wave of relief washed over me. I could finally breathe. The breathing room allowed me to be a better partner and bonus mom, and that's what most people miss about freak-outs: They aren't failures; they're wake-up calls.

Here's the thing—my freak-out worked, not because I was right to explode and not because yelling is an effective communication strategy (it's not), but because underneath all that anger was a real need being completely ignored. My subtle hints weren't working. My attempts to be respectful and not overbearing weren't being heard. So my nervous system did what nervous systems do: It shut down the performance and told the truth in the only way that would get through. And sometimes, you need that.

Damon agreed to take Bruno to the office during virtual school and followed through, and suddenly, I had breathing room. I had space to be human again, which allowed me to be a better partner and bonus mom. That's not weakness; that's wisdom. What I've learned is that freak-outs don't come out of nowhere. They're the end result of a long chain of unspoken needs, ignored hints, and silence masquerading as patience. When you lose it, you're not losing control; you're finally letting someone see how much you need them to understand something. Every freak-out I had in those early condo years (and the first several living in our new home)—and there were plenty—wasn't really about the dishes or the pee on the floor or who got credit for the lightsaber. Underneath it all was the same message: "I matter. My effort matters. My needs matter. And I'm not going to keep performing like they don't." Damon and the kids needed to hear that, and honestly, I needed to hear that about myself. My freak-out about being trapped in the condo wasn't...

Actually, the condo wasn't the issue; control was. It was about not being asked what I needed and the fundamental unfairness of managing the fallout from Damon's parenting choices. Once I understood this deeply, I could communicate differently in the future, not because my anger disappeared, but because I understood its source. The night of my profanity-filled rant, I didn't immediately feel better; I felt embarrassed, like I'd failed at being the "good bonus mom," and proved myself difficult and ungrateful. But this is where Disney Dad shone.

Damon didn't say much that night, just "okay." The next day, however, after he and Bruno came home from his office, he smiled and asked, "How was your day, princess? Do you feel better?" That was all I needed: validation, understanding, and action. He provided it, perhaps with some initial resentment toward my approach, but he didn't hold it against me. That's what real partnership looks like when navigating the bonus mom journey—not perfect, but real. In the end, the challenges we faced in my condo became stepping stones toward a deeper understanding of ourselves and each other. Those moments of tension transformed into opportunities for growth. Each time I was pushed to my limit, I discovered the strength to voice my needs, advocate for my space, and embrace the chaos of blended family life. Now, I see those freak-outs not as failures but as necessary catalysts for change. They remind me that it's okay to speak up and express my feelings, that vulnerability can lead to connection, and that my voice matters just as much as everyone else's.

Let's be clear, ladies: you heard correctly when I mentioned "those freak-outs." You *will* experience more than one during this journey—several, in fact. I've had more than I can count, and that's okay. When these moments happen, remind yourself that you're not a bad bonus mom or a bad mom. You're human, and our emotional—sometimes over-the-top—reactions help us release pent-up feelings. They're important for our well-being.

You're still a badass, and you're still amazing. Giving yourself grace, patience, and understanding is what makes you an empowering force.

Embrace the truth in your emotions. As you navigate the ups and downs of family life, remember that your feelings are valid, and your voice is essential. Each moment of tension isn't just a challenge; it's an opportunity to illuminate your needs and foster deeper connections. When you honor your emotions, you pave the way for understanding and growth—not just for yourself, but for your entire family. So, let your voice rise above the chaos; let it be a powerful reminder that you deserve a space where your needs are acknowledged and celebrated. In this beautiful, messy journey, every emotional truth you embrace brings you one step closer to a richer, more authentic family dynamic. Embrace the journey, for it is in these moments that you truly find your strength and your place.

Love Them Like You Mean It

Happy birthday, Michelle!
Hope you have a great day! Love you! Bruno

Loving someone else's kids can be different than you expect. You arrive ready to embrace them, but then reality sets in. You're tired, frustrated, and sometimes it feels like nothing you do makes a difference. Amidst the chaos, it's easy to forget the simplest thing: to just love them. But showing love requires intention, especially when you're running on empty.

Early on with Bruno, I was so focused on proving myself as the perfect bonus mom that I lost sight of what truly mattered—connecting with him. I was caught up in grocery shopping, managing schedules, and enforcing rules. I was parenting from a place of control instead of love, and he felt it. That moment was my wake-up call. I had to shift my approach, starting with being truly present—not just physically there while scrolling my phone, but engaging with him. I began asking about his day and genuinely listening, noticing when he came home with a heaviness and offering to talk. I put my phone down during dinner to focus on my family.

Love shows up in small moments: a hug when Rocco visits, stocking some of his favorite snacks, or sitting with Bruno when he's upset about something—not trying to fix it, just listening. I learned that these gestures communicate what words often cannot: "You matter to me."

Of course, there will be days when you feel stretched thin, and loving them might feel like just another item on your to-do list. On those days, it's important to give yourself permission to be human while still showing up. One day, I snapped at Bruno over homework—not because of anything he did, but because I was burned out. The look on his face broke my heart, and in that moment, I realized I had been so focused on doing the right thing that I had forgotten to simply love him—the uncomplicated kind of love that shows up, pays attention, and genuinely cares. I paused, took a breath, and said, "I'm sorry. I'm frustrated about something unrelated, and I took it out on you. That wasn't okay." Acknowledging my mistake not only repaired our connection but also showed him that recognizing our flaws and apologizing is an essential part of love.

In a blended family, love means showing these kids they matter, even amid complexity. It's about celebrating their achievements—not because it's your role, but because you genuinely care. It's remembering what they shared and asking about it later, proving you were truly listening. Quality time is where the magic happens. It's not about Instagram-perfect moments but real connections: movie nights where you're genuinely watching together, conversations over dinner with thoughtful questions, or walks where they share their day—these are the moments when they feel most loved. Encouragement is powerful—not the generic "good job," but genuine recognition. "I noticed how calmly you handled that situation; that's really mature." "I love how thoughtful you are with your friends."

Kids can tell the difference between empty praise and sincere acknowledgment. The hardest lesson for me was realizing that loving them doesn't mean always being available or perfect. Sometimes it means saying, "I need a break, but I love you." It can mean acknowledging that you're not equipped to help with something and finding someone who is. Sometimes, it's about sitting with them in their difficult feelings instead of trying to fix them. Kids in blended families navigate so much: divided loyalties, routine changes, and complex family dynamics. They're trying to figure out where they fit and if they're loved despite it all.

In high school, Bruno participated in *The Spartan Edition*, a daily 7- to 10-minute news program broadcast to the entire student body. The show covered everything from school events and sports to politics, lighthearted stories, weather, and fundraising. I loved watching Bruno grow more confident on screen throughout the year. Whether he appeared on camera or worked behind the scenes, I made an effort to watch, engage with, and share my enthusiasm for his work. I would often ask him about his segments, discussing what went well and what he might change. This became a special connection for us, as I was also podcasting weekly with my sister, Tanya. In addition to attending his lacrosse games, supporting his involvement with *The Spartan Edition* was another way I showed him love and attention for the things he cared about.

Your role as a bonus mom isn't to consistently answer questions with a resounding "yes"; it's to show them that you love them not despite the complications, but in the midst of them. It doesn't have to be complicated. Cook their favorite meal. Ask about their day. Show up for their games. Listen when they talk. Celebrate their wins and hold space for their struggles. Be the adult who loves them as they are. That's what Badass Bonus Moms do: We love these kids like we mean it, especially on the tough days.

Sharing Is Caring

Happy Valentine's Day!
I'm in class right now I'll call you after.
Love you so much! Bruno

When you become a bonus mom, no one prepares you for the sheer amount of sharing involved. It's not just your space or your time; it's your energy, emotional capacity, and even your finances! Somehow, though, you adjust. You eventually fall in love with those kids as if they were your own, and that feeling is priceless. Yet, nothing quite prepares you for the time warp, akin to living in a college dorm where boundaries are as nonexistent as your study schedule. Ah, the joys of sharing a fridge with a roommate who treats your snacks like a buffet! Transitioning from solo living—where your precious snacks are safe from being "borrowed" without permission—to sharing your home can feel like starring in your own sitcom. You come home to find someone sprawled out on your couch, flipping through channels and asking a million questions before you've even had the chance to take off your shoes. If you already have kids of your own, you might be used to this behavior, but if you don't, brace yourself for a longer adjustment period than you anticipated.

When Damon first moved in, our transition was smooth sailing. Why wouldn't it be? I adore spending time with him. We share similar tastes in movies and shows, and he *is* kind, funny, smart, and, let's be honest, very sexy. For a while, it felt like we were too busy enjoying each other's company to even notice the TV. Ah, those blissful days when I was the main priority!

But then things changed. Let's be real: while change can be stressful, you eventually learn to roll with it. Yet, having your groceries mysteriously disappear like a bad magic trick? Not so fun. Ladies, I get it—sharing is caring. But what do you do when you didn't sign up for it?

When Bruno first moved in, Damon took charge of the grocery shopping. We'd ask the boys what they liked, which was a moving target since their preferences changed daily. I'd tag along to understand their tastes better, but let's just say grocery trips became a game of culinary roulette. Rocco, who lived with his mom, had a tough time expressing his preferences, which made things even trickier. As we shopped, we'd toss in a few "adult" treats—dairy-free ice cream and truffle-flavored pretzels, the essentials. When I craved one of those items and it was mysteriously gone, my first thought was, "Damon probably ate it." No big deal, I figured; he's my partner.

After we moved from a condo to a house, I found myself doing most of the grocery shopping. Little did I know that shopping for two extra people—and three when Rocco was over—was far pricier than my solo budget. And if you bring your bonus kids along, expect that grocery bill to skyrocket as they toss things in your cart like little starving gremlins. Instead of stressing over the hefty bill, I'd cheer myself up by snagging a few treats:

my beloved dairy-free ice cream, organic cold-pressed juice, gluten-free crackers, and some snacks for Damon. Back home, I'd call for the boys to help unload the car, pleased with my haul. But then, the mystery began. Week after week, I noticed my hard-earned items disappearing. I naturally assumed it was Damon, annoying but not a huge deal. After several months, I finally snapped. "Babe, can you please let me know if you finish my organic juice or fancy cheese? A heads-up would be nice!" Damon looked bewildered. "What are you talking about?" he asked. "One of the boys probably drank or ate it," he replied casually. Wait, what? Why would they drink or eat something I bought without asking? Damon had an open-fridge policy with his ex: anything in the fridge was fair game for the boys—except alcohol. I was floored. My dad had a stash of Breyers vanilla ice cream practically locked behind a vault door; we knew better than to touch it unless offered. Basic rule: if you didn't buy it, you don't eat it. "You're telling me your kids are drinking my nine-dollar organic juice?!" I exclaimed, incredulous. Damon shrugged as if I'd asked him to solve a Rubik's cube. Clearly, this was a battle I wasn't going to win; it was time to establish some ground rules. Ugh!

I sat the boys down and calmly explained that unless I explicitly said they could have something, they needed to ask first. Spoiler alert: this didn't go as planned. They would simply ask Damon, who would always say yes. So, I created a designated shelf in the fridge, labeled it with my name in bold letters, and gathered everyone in the kitchen. "These are my snacks. You are not allowed to touch these unless you ask ME, not your dad, first. Got it?" They all nodded, and miraculously, this reduced the problem. Purchasing groceries still comes with its challenges, especially when Bruno comes home from college or Rocco visits.

Damon often forgets that he just used the last of something I was planning to enjoy. However, I've learned to manage my frustration, focusing instead on the joy of seeing the boys. In the end, sharing truly *is* caring, but only when everyone is on the same page. It can feel disrespectful when someone else makes decisions about what you need without consulting you.

Ladies, embrace the chaos, establish your boundaries, and remember that being a bonus mom is a wild ride—but one worth taking. You're not just sharing space; you're building a family, and that's the most rewarding adventure of all! In the grand scheme of things, remember that every challenge is an opportunity for growth. So keep your head high, your snacks close, and your heart open. You're not just a bonus mom; you're Badass Bonus Moms, and your journey is just beginning!

Listening To Your Intuition

Dear Stephanie, thank you for being very kind and thoughtful of everyone in this family, including me. Merry Christmas or Happy Holidays. Love, Rocco.

Okay, here's something nobody tells you about being a bonus mom: you're going to develop a sixth sense about these kids, and it might freak you out a little. At first, I didn't trust it. Not my instincts—I've always trusted those. But how could I know so deeply when something was either right or wrong with Bruno from the moment we met? I wasn't his mom and didn't have years of history with him. Even though I'm intuitive, clairvoyant, and empathic by nature, I didn't have the "mom instinct" everyone talks about. So, when I felt that nagging sensation that something was off, I second-guessed myself.

But here's what I've learned: that instinct you develop as a bonus mom is real and powerful, and you should listen to it.

It started small. Bruno would come home from school, and something in the way he moved through the door told me his day had been rough—not because he said anything; usually, it was just a quick "Hi, Michelle" before heading to his room. But there was a weight in his shoulders, a dullness in his eyes. I felt a pull in my chest that whispered, "Go talk to him."

The first few times I acted on that feeling, I hesitated. What if he thought I was being too nosy? He was a young teenager, not one of my Love Clients. What if he told his dad I was overstepping? What if I was wrong, and he was fine, making it all weird?

But I decided to trust that feeling, and each time, I was right. One afternoon, I remember him coming home with that familiar heaviness about him. I took a breath and, in what felt like a risk, asked about his day—not with the usual, surface-level question that elicits a "fine," but with genuine curiosity. I showed him I cared about what was going on in his world. He brushed me off at first, a classic teenage deflection, but I didn't push; I simply left space.

Eventually, he came back and sat down. "It was rough," he admitted. "There's a lot of drama in our friend group." And just like that, we had a conversation that mattered—not because I had the answers, but because I was present. I noticed, and I showed him that even though I'm not his mom, I'm someone who sees him and cares enough to ask. That's when I realized something crucial: this instinct isn't about having the right to know what's going on; it's about the connection you've built.

It's about showing up consistently and loving your bonus kids enough that you naturally attune to the shifts in their energy. You pick up on the subtle cues—the way they walk, the tone of their voice, the energy they bring into a room. Your antenna is up. The longer you're in this role, the stronger this instinct becomes.

It's not mystical; it's what happens when you pay attention to someone consistently, when you love them, when you show up for them without expecting anything in return.

But let's be real: there were times I doubted myself. I'd wonder, "Am I overstepping? Is it my place to notice this? What if I'm wrong?" That's the paradox of being a bonus mom, right? You're expected to care enough to show up, but not so much that you're trying to replace their actual mom. It's a tightrope walk. You learn to navigate it by trusting your gut and allowing your actions to speak for themselves. When Bruno realized I wasn't trying to fix everything or take over—that I was just there, present and attuned—he started to trust that I was safe. My instincts came from a place of genuine love, not control.

The more I trusted my intuition, the stronger it became.

I remember when Bruno came home during his first year of college for the weekend. We were all at dinner, and something felt off with him. His laugh sounded forced; his stories lacked their usual spark. I could sense that something weighed heavily on him. After dinner, when he was in his room, I went to check on him. The moment we were alone, I gently asked, "What's going on? You seem a little distant." And then he opened up—college stress, friend dynamics, work assignments, all the burdens he was carrying that night at dinner. We talked for over thirty minutes. I didn't try to fix it; I just listened. I let him know I saw what he was dealing with. That conversation meant everything—not because I solved his problems, but because I noticed something was wrong and cared enough to ask.

So, know this: that instinct you're developing? It's not overstepping. It's you being attuned to someone you love. In the context of being a bonus mom—someone who doesn't have a biological claim and has to earn her place every single day—this attunement is your greatest strength. You're reading the room. You're paying attention. You're showing these kids that they matter.

It's powerful when someone notices even the slightest shift—that's love in action. You'll have moments of self-doubt, wondering if you're doing too much or not enough, worrying about crossing a line. But I promise you, when your instincts stem from genuine care, kids feel it. They can tell the difference between someone genuinely checking in and someone being controlling. They know when you're showing up for them versus trying to insert yourself into their lives.

So trust that gut feeling. Listen to that voice that says something's off. Follow that instinct that prompts you to make their favorite snack or ask the real question instead of a surface-level one. You're becoming the kind of bonus mom who matters—not because you're their mother, but because you're engaged, present, and willing to care. The bonus moms who make the biggest impact aren't the ones who try to be mom; they're the trusted adults who see them, who notice, who care enough to ask. You're building something here. Every time you trust your instincts and show up for these kids, you're proving you deserve a seat at the table—not because you gave birth to them, but because you showed up, paid attention, and loved them when you didn't have to.

Ladies, that instinct is real, so trust it. Watch how it transforms your relationship with these kids. You've got this. Your Badass Bonus Moms gut knows exactly what it's doing. Embrace it, and let it guide you as you build those invaluable connections. This journey will be filled with challenges, but with your intuition as your ally, you're more than capable of navigating it with grace and love.

The Priority Shift

There's an undeniable thrill at the start of a new relationship. Dressing up, you feel excited whether he's taking you out or you're going to his place. When a guy puts in the effort—planning dates, surprising you with home-cooked meals, sending flirty texts, and whisking you away on weekend getaways—you feel like a top priority.

But then you become a bonus mom, and suddenly, that priority list feels rewritten without your input. Your partner's kids should absolutely be a top priority, but when you go from being his shining star to feeling like an afterthought, it stings. The transition from sexy boyfriend to dad is palpable. The man who once woke up beside you, brewing coffee and inviting you to cuddle, now seems to have forgotten you exist. Instead, he's flipping pancakes for the kids, leaving you to fend for yourself.

I'll never forget the times when we had both Bruno and Rocco. I'd walk into the kitchen and see Damon cooking breakfast for his kids. Seeing him cook is undeniably sexy, but the charm fades when you realize you're making your own breakfast. And when he serves the kids first, it feels like you've been demoted from partner to invisible roommate.

It's tough to watch the man who once catered to your every whim focus entirely on his kids. Don't get me wrong; I love how devoted Damon is to his boys, but it took him longer than I expected to find a balance that included me.

Having no children of my own, Damon was still my top priority. Making him feel special was second nature, so why wasn't I receiving the same treatment? Weeks passed where our kitchen conversations felt less like intimate moments and more like family meetings about meals and games. When he suggested a family vacation—all of us crammed into one room—I recoiled. I wasn't ready to share a room, let alone a bed, with his boys in the bed next to ours. Instead of shrinking into the background, I realized that his life with his ex was vastly different from the one we were trying to build. We needed to consciously prioritize each other, especially since I didn't have a history with his kids. I share this because it's crucial to remember that many men are oblivious to these subtle shifts. Never assume; communication is key, and your feelings are valid, no matter how insignificant they seem.

After weeks of feeling sidelined, I finally spoke up. Damon looked genuinely surprised, clearly unaware that he had unintentionally displaced me. Once he understood, everything began to change. He started asking, "What do you want for breakfast? How about pancakes?" Although he still served the kids first, I helped dish out the plates, which felt less like a demotion and more like a shared effort. And we made sure to schedule regular date nights, giving me something to look forward to amidst the chaos. Here's the thing: It's essential to maintain your status as a priority within this new family dynamic. You're not just a bonus mom helping out; you're a vital part of the equation and deserve to be valued. The right partner will listen and adjust to ensure you feel cherished. Priorities will shift, especially with kids. But remember, a changing list doesn't mean you've been relegated to the bottom.

Creating a dynamic where everyone feels included, loved, and valued—that's what being Badass Bonus Moms means. Let's support each other, communicate openly, and ensure that no one feels left out in this beautifully chaotic family life. Embrace the shifts, celebrate the chaos, and remember that being a priority is about mutual respect and love. You're not just navigating a new relationship; you're building a blended family, and that's a journey worth celebrating!

Navigating the Complexity of Disney Dad

*Happy Mother's Day! I bet Chloe is very happy
to have you as her adopted mother!*
Bruno

Being a bonus mom is already challenging. Now, add a "Disney Dad" into the mix: the guy who enters every room radiating fun and excitement, like he just stepped off a magic carpet, ready to turn an ordinary Tuesday into a day at Disneyland. His mission? To be the "fun dad" 99.8% of the time. And while he may have perfected the art of saying "yes," actual parenting often takes a backseat, adding more stress for you.

When it comes to decisions, Disney Dad says "yes" faster than a kid can finish the question. "Can we get ice cream?" "Yes!" "Can we stay up late?" "Yes!" "Can I have a pet tiger?" "Well, let's see what we can do!" Meanwhile, homework, chores, and tests vanish into thin air like Cinderella at midnight. The kids come running in with sparkling eyes, and there he is—arms wide open, ready to make their wildest dreams come true.

You might think, "Honey, can we pause the fun? I'd like to discuss boundaries." But try getting a word in when he's busy being the life of the party.

Here's the reality: being Disney Dad is exhausting—but not for him. You're the one picking up the slack, enforcing rules while he's off gallivanting in the land of "YES!" You become the voice of reason in a room full of children, which somehow makes you the cranky one. And when he's not around, the kids test every boundary he's never set. The questions keep coming: "Dad said we could have pizza and a movie." "Dad said I can stay up late on a school night to watch basketball." "Dad said yes, so why are you saying no?"

There it is. You've become the bad guy—again. Ugh. Your partner probably thinks, "What's the harm in being fun?" It's understandable. We all want our kids to have a good time and make memories. But here's the thing: too much fun without structure creates chaos—and forces you to become the enforcer. Disciplining a child? Not fun. Setting boundaries? Definitely not on his itinerary. So guess who gets to play the killjoy? You: the not-so-fun girlfriend or partner who suddenly has to be the taskmaster while he gets to be the hero. The dynamic shifts quickly. You want to create a nurturing environment, but it's difficult when the other adult is handing out candy like it's going out of style or acting like a teenager to connect with his kids. You didn't sign up to parent a grown man and his children. The kids start to understand the game: When you say no, they go to him. When he says yes, you're the obstacle, the one who doesn't understand how much fun they deserve. This was an epic battle in our home when Bruno was living with us before he went to college.

Damon and I would have disagreements—putting it nicely—when he would consistently say yes to Bruno without asking if he had homework or checking his grades, which, at one point, were subpar! This wasn't Bruno's norm as a straight-A student, but Damon wanted to be the cool dad. I understood, but I also knew it wasn't appropriate at that age. So, what's a bonus mom to do? Besides running for the hills—because let's be real, that's tempting—communicate as best you can, not just a one-time conversation, but a real, ongoing dialogue about what parenting actually looks like. Of course, have this conversation when things are calm—not in the middle of a meltdown. "I love how you bring joy to the kids' lives; they need that. But I'm noticing I'm the one enforcing consequences while you're making all the big promises. How can we balance this together?" Sounds easy, but let's be real; it's not easy when you're frustrated and smoke is coming out of your ears. The "pleasant" conversations I tried to have with Damon were often laced with resentment and frustration, and believe me, he could hear it in my tone. In Damon's defense (not making excuses), he really wasn't aware he was being a "Disney Dad"—until I pointed it out.

Most men don't realize the impact of their actions. He thought he was creating fun memories, but in doing so, he was inadvertently complicating our parenting dynamic. While he believed he was being a good parent—which he was—however, instilling basic respect for me and our home is equally important. Every household is unique, and every child is different. You might have a partner who is stricter than you feel he should be, or a "Disney Dad" who knows when to have fun but also balances responsibility. You might even have a partner who expects you to do all the work. There's no one-size-fits-all action plan; it's about communicating how you feel, not letting resentment fester and get out of control, and speaking up for your own sanity and well-being. Being a bonus mom means figuring out what works for you, period. You cannot change a man if he doesn't want to change. Damon and I had to have multiple conversations about his "Disney Dad" approach. Although he didn't completely change, he definitely heard me. Over time—and after having to parent on his own when I was dealing with health issues—he realized and adjusted his approach.

Ladies, you don't have to choose between being fun and being respected. You can be both—but only if your partner shows up as a real co-parent, not just a fun-dispensing machine. Kids need structure and consistency. They need to know that when you say something, it matters. Your partner needs to understand that supporting you supports them—it supports the whole family. So, have those conversations and set those boundaries. And remember: if he can't step up as a real parent, that's not a reflection on you. Decide if this is a battle and character flaw you can live with or not. You are the only one who knows the answer.

Stephanie, I wanted you to know that you are so important to my life. You were brought to me when I needed you the most. I am working on being the BEST MAN I can be. But, there would be a hole in me without the person who makes me one.
I so appreciate you and all that you are.
My life and the boys is so much better with you.
You complete our HOUSE and LIVES..

You are my Love!

You are my Lifetime Partner!

You are my Inspiration!

You are my Complete Heart!

You are my Beautiful!
You are the Best Thing In My Life!!!
Let's work even harder to be spiritually
& emotionally THE BEST COUPLE EVER!
**Mixed in with being a power couple & lots of continued*
physical connection.
I Love you! Damon

Navigating different parenting styles is not just normal; it can enrich your family dynamic. Embrace these differences. For example, a "Disney Dad," when paired with a more structured parenting style, can bring balance to the household in unexpected ways. These fun moments can calm the chaos, relieve stress, and create a vibrant atmosphere for both the kids and you. Your ability to create structure and consistency complements his fun-loving nature, allowing for a more harmonious household. Remember, you're not alone in this journey. It's okay to feel overwhelmed sometimes, but know that you're building something wonderful. With open communication and mutual respect, you can navigate these complexities together and create a loving and supportive environment for everyone.

When She Won't Acknowledge You

Dear Stephanie, Merry Christmas and a Happy New Year! Thank you for always trying to help out with everything and being selfless. Love, Rocco.

The lacrosse field buzzed on a Saturday morning in spring. Standing on the sidelines with Damon and Bruno, I cheered for Rocco, feeling every bit the Badass Bonus Mom. Then, his ex walked onto the sidelines, and I sensed the shift in energy before I even turned to look. That's how present she was—not physically close, but undeniably there. The vibe changed instantly. Damon nodded when he spotted her, and then her eyes landed on me. I watched her assess my presence—standing next to her ex-husband and oldest son, cheering for Rocco in a way that felt both proprietary and permanent. She looked away, a deliberate dismissal, as if I didn't exist. Ouch! Bruno looked at us. "Is it okay if I go say hi to Mom?" he asked. Did he feel he needed our permission? I felt uncomfortable and sad that Bruno was caught in the middle. "Of course," we both said in unison. After the game, Damon needed to grab Rocco's overnight bag from his ex's car. I stood awkwardly while she and Damon discussed logistics. She never acknowledged me—not a single "hi" or nod. I was invisible. I remember thinking, she hasn't even officially met me! Why isn't Damon introducing us? We're going to be in each other's lives forever. How could she be okay with not meeting the woman who lives with her son full-time? I hesitated to intrude while she and Damon discussed exchange times for Rocco, who lived with her. Bruno and Rocco were right there, and I didn't want to create a scene—her body language clearly conveyed, "Back off!" Yikes! Even without words, her energy spoke volumes.

Over the following months, I extended several olive branches. I took trips to the mall with Bruno to help him pick out gifts for his mom—birthday, Christmas, and Mother's Day gifts—and I paid for them. I wrote her a note thanking her for sharing her boys with me. I attempted to connect with her by giving gifts: a candle for Mother's Day (through Bruno), a bottle of wine at Christmas, and champagne for her birthday. I even gave her an expensive pet bed, which my cat never used, but she happily took; her sons have told me numerous times that their mom's cat and little dog love it and use it daily. Despite all this, I never received a thank you or any acknowledgment. The worst part wasn't the rejection itself, but the confusion it sowed. What was I waiting for? Her approval? Permission to be part of this family? Seriously? It felt absurd, and I was exhausted from waiting.

As much as I loved her boys, this dynamic wasn't worth my energy. Then, eleven months after we moved into our new home, Damon's ex arrived to pick up Rocco and her dog, which we'd watched for the weekend. I was in the kitchen when she came, and something inside me snapped. Grabbing the dog, I walked outside, opened the passenger door of her car, and said, "Hi, I'm Stephanie." I extended my hand before she could pretend I wasn't there. "I know we haven't *officially* met, but I wanted to introduce myself. Thank you for letting us watch your dog, and thank you for sharing your amazing boys with me. I truly feel blessed." She looked genuinely shocked—as if she never expected me to exist, to claim space, to say my own name. She shook my hand, managed a "hello" for the first time, and I handed her the dog before walking away. I didn't need a long conversation; I just needed her to know I existed, that I was here to stay, and that I wouldn't wait for permission to be part of this family. I was going to define myself.

Here's something nobody prepares you for: your partner's ex isn't just an inconvenience. She's a person who knows your partner in ways you don't. She created memories with him, shares children with him, and is a significant part of his history. When Damon talked about Bruno and Rocco's mom, it was clear: she's a good mother. She loves her sons deeply and is an incredible cook—Bruno and Rocco rave about her meals as if she invented food. She loves skiing and camping with the boys, plans trips, and shows up for them in real ways. Yet, when I'm less than a foot away, she won't even look at me? Eye roll.

Ladies, here's the thing about blending families that nobody talks about: you're not just dealing with your partner's past relationship; you're dealing with the person *from* that past relationship—a person who might feel threatened by you, angry at you, or who simply decided, before ever meeting you, that she wouldn't like you. You don't get a choice in this, and neither does she. What frustrated me wasn't that she would always be in our lives—that was expected. It was how easily she could change plans (pick-up times, holiday schedules, etc.) without a second thought, but if *we* needed or wanted to change something, she'd lose it. Her actions were childish: last-minute changes, refusing to text Damon back in a timely manner, and communicating only through abrupt messages. Damon rarely addressed it. I'd bring it up repeatedly: "This is frustrating. Can you talk to her about giving us more notice?" He'd brush it off: "She's just stressed about work." So I was left feeling dismissed—not just by his ex, but by my own partner. Ugh.

The breaking point came when Damon's kids repeatedly told me their mom didn't like me, and shared other negative comments. Adding to this, I saw multiple text messages from his ex containing negative remarks about me—yet she never voiced these concerns to my face despite numerous opportunities at the kids' games. Even after I'd sent a letter and a text suggesting we meet for coffee, she remained silent. So, I took the low road, and I'm not proud of it. I'm sharing this because it's an important part of my bonus mom journey. There were times I trash-talked Damon's ex in front of the boys—not constantly, but often enough. When frustrated, hurt, or feeling dismissed by her actions, those feelings would explode out of my mouth before I could stop them. I was angry and would tell Damon, "When she sends you a disrespectful text about me, you need to address it. Not just for me—for us, and for the kids. If they see you allowing her to treat me poorly, they'll think it's acceptable behavior, and that my role here is secondary." I'd also make sarcastic remarks, intending them to be funny, but they were just mean. I watched the boys' faces shift each time. They weren't angry, just uncomfortable. And who could blame them? I was forcing them to choose between their mother and the woman trying to build a life with their father. That wasn't fair.

I only know one side of the story regarding Damon and his ex-wife's marriage: what didn't work, how he felt, and why it ended. Damon told me he tried multiple times to reconcile, but she was non-responsive. He spent time after work hanging out with friends, sleeping on the couch, or in one of his sons' rooms. He and his ex-wife stopped sharing a bedroom and only spoke when necessary, living like roommates for over two years before I met him. However, I don't know her story, what she felt, and why she pulled away from Damon. I was so caught up in being a bonus mom that I forgot to have compassion for the woman who brought two amazing boys into this world and now into my life. So, I stopped trying to win. I stopped competing with her in my head. I stopped keeping score about who the kids liked better, who they talked about more, or whose cooking they preferred. I stopped using the kids as evidence in my case against her. Something shifted—not with her. She was still distant, still communicating only through text to Damon, still creating tension, but with me—with how I moved through this space, with my own sense of purpose. I was a consistent, caring adult in these kids' lives. That was it—not a replacement for their mother, not a competitor, just someone who showed up.

Although Damon didn't love these conversations about how I felt regarding all the dismissive texts his ex-wife sent over the years, it meant he couldn't just be the nice guy trying to keep the peace; he had to take a stance. And he did, not perfectly, not every time, but he started checking her when she was out of line. He backed me up when she tried to undermine decisions we'd made. He began protecting the boundary that said: You're my partner, and this family includes her too. This mattered more than her looking at me, accepting me, or becoming my friend. Did his ex-wife do some things better than me? Absolutely. She was an extraordinary cook and planned great camping and ski trips—things that aren't my forte. She had a history with them I will never have, but I brought different things. I was there on school nights, helped with homework assignments, was there through the growing pains, attended multiple orthodontist and doctor's appointments over the years, and most importantly, I have helped shape and mold Bruno into the young man he is today. I was present in the mundane moments that actually build relationships. I was creating my own memorable moments, and that was all that mattered.

As Bruno's bonus mom, scheduling his doctor's appointments was part of my role. Even after he had lived with us for over four years, I continued to schedule his appointments as I always had, despite him being seventeen. Then, his ex discovered this and emailed the doctor, asserting that I lacked the authority to schedule appointments. She insisted that she—who didn't live with Bruno, wasn't aware of his daily schedule, and wasn't managing his life—needed to handle his medical decisions. Reading that email triggered a shift within me—not exactly anger, but a sense of resignation. I finally understood the dynamic I was dealing with. Three weeks later, she emailed the doctor again, this time saying I could *now* schedule appointments, as if I had been waiting for her permission and should be grateful for it. When Damon told me, I just shook my head and laughed. I realized the real battle wasn't between her and me, but within myself: the part of me tempted to be petty versus the part of me committed to being present. I chose the latter, even—especially— when it was difficult.

Eight months later, the week after my surgery, Rocco had his first freshman homecoming dance. Despite still being in pain, I insisted that Damon and I drive the two hours to the mountain venue where Rocco and his friends were meeting for pre-dance photos. Determined to capture some great shots of Rocco, his date, and their group, I moved slowly and took numerous pictures. The next day, Damon's ex contacted him, explaining that the sunlight had ruined her photos and asked if he could send her any he had taken. Since I had taken almost all of them, I immediately forwarded them to her. Predictably, I received no acknowledgment—no thank you, heart emoji, or even a thumbs up. But that's just her; her anger is her burden. Through this experience, I learned that a good relationship with his ex didn't depend on Damon defending me. Instead, a healthy family system required him not to undermine me. I had to be explicit about this with him, not with anger, but with clarity.

The hardest part about being Badass Bonus Moms isn't the ex, per se, but the undefined, uncomfortable space where you're both trying to define your relationship. Are you enemies? Hopefully not. Are you friends? That's probably unrealistic. Are you cordial co-parents? Maybe, eventually. For now, you're somewhere in between—something without a name or clear job description. That ambiguity is a challenge in itself.

I've accepted that Damon's ex may never fully accept me, that she might always see me as the woman who came after her, who now occupies space in her ex-husband's life and has access to her children in ways she doesn't. And you know what? That's okay. I don't need her approval to know who I am. I don't need her to see me at lacrosse games for me to exist in this family. I don't need her to like me, invite me to things, or become my friend. What I need is for her to respect that I'm here, that I'm part of her children's lives, and that I'm not going anywhere. I need my partner to protect that boundary. Everything else is just noise.

But here's the truth: being a Badass Bonus Mom is about

more than navigating the complexities of your partner's past; it's about stepping into your power and owning your place in the family. You're not just an add-on, but a vital part of the tapestry weaving their lives together. Embrace your role with confidence, and show up for the children with love, understanding, and resilience. Your presence matters, even if unacknowledged at times, because you are creating a safe space for them to thrive, and that is invaluable. If you find yourself feeling invisible or dismissed, remember that you are more than enough. You are building relationships that will stand the test of time, teaching the children that love comes in many forms. Each day, you define what it means to be a family, one moment at a time. Keep shining your light, and trust that, in time, your efforts will bear fruit. You are a force to be reckoned with, and your journey—though challenging—is shaping a beautiful legacy for everyone involved.

Igniting Self-Love Through Forgiveness

love you Michelle, Bruno

Forgiveness is one of the most powerful tools in your toolkit as Badass Bonus Moms. Let's be real: you're going to make mistakes. No one is perfect, and stepping into this role can be incredibly challenging—especially when you had no idea what you were signing up for. You're balancing expectations from your partner, navigating relationships with kids who aren't biologically yours, and doing it all without a roadmap. Mistakes and bumps in the road are part of the deal, and embracing this uncharted territory with an open heart can transform everything.

Being kind to yourself and forgiving your partner's kids for their slip-ups is essential. This journey isn't just about you; it's a shared experience that thrives on empathy and understanding.

I understand that forgiveness can be challenging. When I was younger, I thought forgiving someone meant accepting their behavior and, even worse, that it made me the weaker person.

In truth, forgiving someone is about reclaiming your power. It doesn't mean you have to accept their behavior moving forward or keep that person in your life.

Equally important is forgiving yourself for the inevitable missteps along the way. Whether it's a moment of frustration where you snap or a decision that didn't turn out as planned, these experiences are simply opportunities for growth.

I remember a family game night that took an unexpected turn. I had high hopes for a fun evening, but when Bruno started joking around instead of following the rules, I lost my cool. "Can you just focus for once?" I shouted, instantly regretting it. The silence that followed felt heavy, and I could see the hurt in Bruno's eyes. In that moment, I realized my frustration had overshadowed my intention to create joy.

After a few moments of reflection, I knew I had to apologize. Kneeling down to his level, I said, "I'm really sorry for raising my voice. My frustration got the best of me. Can we start over?"

That moment taught me that forgiveness as a bonus mom begins with self-awareness: recognizing when you've crossed a line and having the courage to make amends. This simple act not only mended our relationship but also showed Bruno that making mistakes is okay; what truly matters is how we respond. It's equally important to forgive your partner's kids for the things they might say or do that upset you. Children are navigating their own emotions, especially in a blended family, and may lash out or say hurtful things as a way of expressing confusion or frustration.

I recall a time when Bruno, in a moment of teenage angst, told me, "You're not my mom. You don't get to tell me what to do!" Initially, those words stung, but I took a deep breath and reminded myself that he was struggling. Instead of reacting defensively, I chose to respond with empathy: "I know I'm not your mom, and I don't want to replace her. I care about you and want to support you, but we do have some rules."

Forgiveness also extends to your partner's ex, whether it's an ex-wife or the mother of their children. You may hear negative comments directed at you, either directly or through your partner, and they can be infuriating. I've had to remind myself that her words often reflect her own struggles, not my worth as a bonus mom. I remember one tense conversation where the ex made a snide remark about how I was "just the girlfriend." It took everything in me to stay calm, reminding myself that her feelings were valid and that she was navigating her own emotions regarding the blended-family dynamic. Instead of responding with anger, I chose to forgive her negativity and focus on what I could control—my reactions and the environment I wanted to create for Bruno.

Family dynamics can be tricky, especially when well-meaning relatives try to insert themselves into the mix. It's important to forgive family members who may be too involved, causing stress in your relationship with your partner and their kids. I've had to have conversations with Damon's family and explain that, while I appreciated their input, I needed the space to navigate my role as a bonus mom in my own way. Forgiveness isn't a one-time action; it's an ongoing process that requires patience and understanding—both for yourself and others. When you feel hurt or frustrated, take a moment to reflect on the bigger picture: Why are you feeling this way? What's at the root of your frustration?

By practicing forgiveness, you cultivate a more harmonious environment for everyone involved, fostering growth and healing for yourself and the children.

Bruno has occasionally spoken disrespectfully or acted out, likely due to growing pains; however, he has always apologized afterward and remained open to communication.

Nurture an atmosphere where everyone feels safe to express their emotions without fear of judgment. As you continue your journey as Badass Bonus Moms, remember that forgiveness is a vital tool for navigating the complexities of blended family life. Embrace mistakes—both yours and the children's—and choose to forgive. This strengthens relationships and promotes your own growth. Ultimately, the art of forgiveness is about love: self-love, love for your partner, and love for your partner's children. It's about creating a family atmosphere where everyone can thrive, learn, and grow together. So, let go of grudges, embrace imperfections, and remember that you're all in this journey together. Your heart—and your family—will thank you for it.

Find Your Voice, It Matters

Happy Monthly Anniversary. Thanks for opening up, letting me know how much you love me. You are so important to my happiness and fullfillment of my heart!
Love Damon

For the first few months of living with Damon and the boys, I was quieter than usual. Not silent, but definitely not fully present. The thing is, I'm not naturally quiet, nor am I good at holding things in. Early on, though, I convinced myself that my opinion didn't matter, that I didn't have the right to speak up about Damon's kids because they weren't mine. I saw myself as just the dad's live-in girlfriend—a woman in the background, supporting but not really steering. Although much of what I was feeling was valid for a bonus mom, that wasn't the whole picture. Part of me also felt like I hadn't earned the right to have opinions.

So, what did this look like in practice? Mumbling under my breath. My facial expressions said everything—I definitely don't have a poker face, a fact my late dad pointed out very early on. I'd pull Damon aside in our bedroom or wait until we went for a walk to unload whatever was bothering me. I made subtle hints about what I needed instead of asking directly—the kind where you hope they'll just figure it out if you drop enough breadcrumbs. "Oh, you still have that big meeting room? I'm sure Bruno would love to spread out." Translation: I'm drowning and need a break.

It was exhausting. I was trying to be respectful and not over-step, but I was actually making myself invisible. I was teaching these kids that women should shrink themselves to make space for others, that their own needs don't matter as much as keeping the peace. That realization hit me hard.

Finding your voice is so important. There's a cost to staying small, and that cost isn't just to you—it's to your entire family. And finding your voice means more than just speaking.

Ladies, let's be clear: your voice matters. Period. But finding it isn't just about talking louder or being more assertive; it's about recognizing something fundamental: you live here, and you matter. Your perspective deserves to be heard. For me, finding my voice started small. It was telling Damon I wasn't comfortable with certain things in the household, sharing my thoughts on how to handle situations with the boys, and say-ing "yes" when I meant yes and "no" when I meant no, instead of just going along with what seemed easiest. One day, it was even telling Damon's ex, sitting right there in her car, that I existed and was now part of this family. It was uncomfortable as hell, but necessary. When I started participating more in conversations, sharing my perspective without apologizing, and setting boundaries and sticking to them, the dynamic shifted. The boys started listening differently, not because I was louder, but because I was real. I wasn't performing respect anymore; I was commanding it by respecting myself first. The vulnerability is where the real power lives. Ladies, when you speak from an authentic place, not trying to be perfect or prove anything, people listen differently. They really do. You're not performing or managing their emotions; you're just telling the truth, and that truth has power.

Then there's the lightsaber incident...

After many purchased, wrapped, and signed gifts given to both boys over the first few years, I finally lost my cool over a lightsaber. Seriously. A lightsaber. The story that unfolded became the most important lesson about communication I've learned. I had purchased Rocco a Star Wars lightsaber for Christmas. Getting to know Rocco was a slow process—he lived with his mom full-time in the mountains, and I had to be intentional. I'd ask Bruno what his brother loved, what would make him light up. I did the research without Rocco ever knowing I was paying that close attention. I wrapped it carefully and signed the card, "From Dad & Stephanie." Then came Father's Day. Rocco wrote in a card to Damon: "Dad, happy Father's Day. You're the best dad ever! Thank you for always giving me the best gifts. I love my lightsaber. Love, Rocco." Ouch! Standing there reading those words, something inside me just...snapped. Not in a dramatic way, and not immediately.

It wasn't a sudden explosion, but more like a slow crack that goes unnoticed until the whole thing shatters. Let me be clear: I genuinely love seeing how much Bruno and Rocco adore their dad; it truly warms my heart. Damon is an amazing father, and he deserves that recognition. However, in that moment, I realized I had become invisible—not to Damon, and not to myself, but to the child I was trying so hard to connect with. I don't offer gifts, attention, time, or help because I need praise. That's simply not who I am. But when credit is consistently given to someone else over and over again without even a simple acknowledgment, it stings. It makes you feel like your efforts are meaningless, like the time you invested in getting to know your bonus kid(s), the thoughtfulness you put into a gift meant to say, "I see you"—all of it attributed to someone else. And I said nothing—not to Rocco, not at that moment. The lightsaber incident became a masterclass in what NOT to do. I didn't speak up when the card was initially written. Damon didn't correct Rocco at the time, so Rocco learned that Dad gets the credit, and I learned a hard lesson: staying silent about feeling invisible only makes you more so. Yikes!

The real lesson wasn't about the lightsaber itself, but about what happens when you don't advocate for yourself. When I finally addressed the lightsaber situation with Damon, I didn't do it impulsively in the heat of the moment, which would have been messy and reactionary. But I also didn't wait weeks, hoping he would magically understand. Instead, I waited for a calm moment—not immediately after the incident, and not while I was still upset. I waited until I could clearly articulate what was bothering me without my voice shaking or my frustration taking over. Then, I created space—real, distraction-free space. We went for a walk in one of our usual spots, where difficult conversations feel less like interrogations and more like we're facing things together. I started with vulnerability rather than blame. "I need to talk about something that's been weighing on me," I said, "and I need you to just listen for a moment before responding."

When I finally told Damon how the lightsaber situation made me feel, I watched him genuinely listen—not defend, not explain, just listen. "I'm feeling invisible," I said. "I spend all this time picking out gifts that I know they'll love. I wrap them. I sign both our names, and somehow, the credit goes to you." I began to realize that if I didn't speak up, no one would know these gifts also came from me—from me, emphasizing that I know these kids and care about making them feel special. Damon's first response was, "Well, I'm their father, so of course…" Ladies, hold your gasps.

Damon wasn't defensive; he was stating a fact. But he did listen. That's when things shifted because he finally understood the emotional reality, not just the logistics of gift-giving. I was working hard to build connections with these kids, and in my effort to be the "good bonus mom," I was making myself invisible. After that conversation, I didn't just let it go. The next time Rocco came to visit and brought his lightsaber—as he had done every time since he got it—I gently corrected him. "I'm so glad you like the gift your dad and I got you," I said. He looked at me and said, "Dad got this for me." I immediately responded, "No, I actually did. Although your dad does get you great gifts, I work hard to find you gifts that you will like and enjoy, and I add your dad's name since we are a team. However, going forward, that won't be happening." Rocco looked at me, surprised. "Oh, well, then thank you."

Here's what changed after that:

In that single interaction, something shifted. Rocco learned that I do things for him, that I'm not just present—I'm intentionally present. And Damon learned that if he wasn't going to speak up, I would, that I wasn't going to disappear for the sake of "keeping the peace." From that point on, gifts I worked hard to find and purchase? My name is on them. The ones I'm okay with being "from both of us"? Those still have Damon's name added. It might sound petty, but it was actually revolutionary. It was me reclaiming visibility. It was me saying—out loud, for the first time—that my work matters.

If you don't advocate for yourself, no one else will. Finding your voice isn't about winning arguments or proving you're right; it's about something much simpler, yet infinitely more powerful: truly knowing you deserve to take up space in your own life. Badass Bonus Moms, you matter. Your perspective matters. Your effort matters. Your feelings matter. Not eventually, not when you've proven yourself worthy, but now. You live in this house, invest in these kids, show up for your partner, and build something real. All of that deserves to be seen and acknowledged—by them, your partner, and, most importantly, by you. When you speak up, you're not being difficult, ungrateful, or too much. You're being honest, and that honesty transforms a household from a place where someone is invisible to a place where everyone is seen. The boys still tease me about the lightsaber, but they also know that when I do something for them, it comes from me, and that matters more than I can say.

Embrace your power and authenticity. Bonus Moms, remember that your voice is not just a tool for communication; it's a beacon of your identity and worth. Each time you assert yourself, you not only advocate for your needs but also model strength and authenticity for your bonus kids, teaching them the invaluable lesson that it's okay to stand up for oneself and that every voice—especially yours—holds weight in shaping the family dynamic. So, step boldly into your truth, knowing that each time you speak, you're not just claiming your space; you're enriching the tapestry of your family with the vibrant colors of your unique perspective. Own it, and let it shine.

The Switzerland Strategy

Happy birthday, Michelle! Have an extremely rad day!
Love you, and thanks for everything! Bruno

"You're not my mother!" As these magical words hit me as I was leaving Bruno's room, and I instinctively stepped back inside. There he was, a distraught fourteen-year-old lying in bed—the boy I had just grounded. It was clear he was grappling with my role in his life. I sat down on the chair across from him, paused, and took a deep breath. "I know," I said. His confusion deepened, as if he thought he was stating a fact I was unaware of. He stared at me, deer-in-headlights, wondering why I was so calm.

Stepping into your role as a Badass Bonus Mom is like embodying Switzerland: neutral, supportive, and wise. I often remind my partner's son, Bruno, of this.

The notion of being the "better parent" can become an unspoken competition, especially when a divorce isn't mutual. One parent might be in denial, clinging to the past, while the other tries to navigate a new reality. As a bonus mom, it's crucial to remain neutral in this tug-of-war. Embracing the "Switzerland" approach provides clarity and calmness in an often-chaotic situation.

My response was simple: "Although I'm not your parent, please know that I care about you and want to be a supportive and neutral figure in your life. I love you very much, and I always try to make thoughtful decisions with your best interests at heart. I'm not trying to buy your affection or compete with your parents. My goal is to provide stability by maintaining healthy boundaries, holding you accountable, and offering guidance when you need it. You may not appreciate it now, but I hope you'll understand someday." I looked Bruno in the eyes and asked if we were okay. His simple "yes" touched me deeply. I stood up, reminded him that I loved him, and hearing him say it back filled me with joy. These moments of connection remind us that we're in this together, building a bond that will only grow stronger.

Don't get me wrong, ladies. Though I had prepared myself to hear Bruno say those words one day, preparing isn't the same as actually hearing them. Of course, my feelings were hurt, and my ego bruised. However, his statement was factually true. But those facts don't negate my being there, loving him and his brother, and enacting my "see something, say something" policy to run a safer home, both mentally and emotionally.

When faced with a "Disney Dad" scenario—where the other parent leans heavily into fun while sidestepping responsibilities—your role becomes even more vital. Being "Switzerland" means you can create a unique bond with your partner's children, different from what they experience with their parents. You're not just another adult; you're a steady presence who can navigate the emotional waters with grace and without demanding perfection. Let's be clear: this doesn't mean you won't lose your cool or drop an F-bomb. Nor does it mean you'll always say the right thing or won't need your own down-time. You're human, not a walking, talking robot.

The more you implement The Switzerland Strategy, the safer your bonus kids will feel, knowing that you're listening, noticing, and not afraid to hold them accountable.

For example, Bruno came home upset after a tough day at school. Instead of brushing it off or distracting him with a fun activity, I sat down with him and asked, "What's going on? You seem upset." He initially shrugged, but with a little gentle prodding, he opened up about feeling left out by his friends and the pressure of having two separate friend groups.

His vulnerability allowed me to offer support. "It's okay to feel that way," I said. "Have you thought about talking to them about how you feel?" This kind of open dialogue helped him process his emotions and gave him tools for future interactions.

Being neutral doesn't mean being passive; it's about noticing things that might otherwise go unnoticed, asking the hard questions, and having those crucial conversations. Part of our role as bonus moms is to step in, ensuring that kids don't walk all over us or create unnecessary drama. We offer praise and admiration where it's deserved, but we also hold them accountable. Sometimes, that means grounding them, taking away their phones, TV time, or gaming privileges—even if it means they miss a birthday party or an important event. Clearly, I've done it all. Grounding isn't fun, but it translates to: "I care enough to discipline you and hold you accountable for your actions. You might not like me now, but you'll thank me later."

Divorced parents have a tough job; they're often trying to heal their own hearts while managing the blame and complexity of the situation. In this emotional whirlwind, they may overlook the signs of what their child is expressing through actions—like tempers flaring, stealing, elusive behavior, or even withdrawal. It's in these moments that the Switzerland parenting style becomes particularly effective for me as a bonus mom.

I've learned to trust my intuition and "spidey sense" regarding Bruno and have become very attuned to his needs. To have a productive conversation, we need to eliminate distractions, as with most children: phones down, TV and video games off, earbuds out, and direct eye contact is a must. I also emphasize that the consequences he faces now are minor compared to those he'll encounter as an independent adult, where failing to meet responsibilities could result in losing a job, car, driver's license, or even his home.

Being "Switzerland" isn't just about neutrality; it's about being a steadfast, loving presence in the lives of my partner's children. It's about understanding that while I'm not their mom, I have the capacity to love them fiercely and guide them gently.

The Switzerland parenting style has been a significant awakening for me. It's taught me that while the role can be challenging, it's also incredibly rewarding. The love I have for Bruno and Rocco fuels my determination to be the best parent figure I can be. Together, we are creating a family dynamic that is unique, filled with love, laughter, and the occasional grounding (let's keep it real).

Badass Bonus Moms, may you embrace your Switzerland spirit, navigate the complexities with grace, and create lasting bonds that will enrich your lives and those of the children you love. You're not just a step-in; you're an integral part of their journey, and that's something truly special.

Be Their Anchor

Love is the essential anchor for bonus kids. As they navigate their emotional landscapes and find their place in a unique family dynamic, they need to feel secure and cherished. Being their anchor isn't just a nice-to-have; it's the foundation upon which everything else is built. Like sponges, children absorb everything around them, both good and bad. When they sense love and support, they flourish; when they feel neglected, it can lead to insecurity and behavioral issues.

Bonus kids have already faced change and the loss of their original family structure. What they need now is consistency, security, and the unwavering knowledge that they are loved. This starts with intentionality; prioritize expressing love openly and frequently. Simple acts of love—hugs, high-fives, saying "I love you," leaving a sweet note in their lunch, or sending a text message telling them how important they are—work wonders and can turn a tough day around. Greeting them with a smile or asking about their day sends a powerful message: "You matter to me." Children need to hear that, especially while navigating the complexities of blended family life.

As a bonus mom, remember that quality time isn't just about being in the same room; it's about being present. Whether you're playing a game, going for a walk, or simply chatting over dinner, those moments foster connection and love. Undivided attention builds trust and security in ways that words alone cannot.

During the pandemic, Damon, Rocco, Bruno, and I started playing countless board games together. We discovered how competitive the boys were at Monopoly and how sharp Bruno was at Clue. We also prioritized sit-down dinners, committing to at least one family meal each week. Those dinners weren't just about food; they were about connection and check-ins. We went for family walks almost daily during the pandemic and afterward, we continued the tradition with walks on Saturdays or Sundays after church.

The boys knew we were there for one another, free from distractions, and that mattered. Being their anchor can be expressed in countless ways, often through actions rather than words. Cook their favorite meal, surprise them with a small treat, help with homework, or attend their games and performances. These gestures show that you care and are invested in their happiness. Children notice and remember these acts, which profoundly impact how they view themselves and their relationships. Encouragement is another powerful tool; children thrive on positive reinforcement. Celebrate their achievements, no matter how small. Did they tie their shoes by themselves? Celebrate! Make a new friend? Celebrate! Pass a test? Celebrate! A little genuine praise can significantly boost their self-esteem and reinforce the idea that they are loved and valued.

There will be days when you feel stretched thin and over-whelmed. You might face tantrums, sibling rivalry, or the general chaos of family life. In those moments, remember that your love is a lifeline. Responding with patience and under-standing instead of frustration models a strong anchor in action, teaching them that love shows up, even when things are hard. Give yourself grace—you're not expected to be perfect. Being their love-anchor is the glue that holds everything together. Children may face challenges—big feelings, changes in rou-tines, and adjusting to new dynamics—but knowing they are unconditionally loved can be a powerful anchor amid the storm. When Bruno lived with us full-time, I made a point to tell him I loved him before he headed to school, went to see a friend, or settled in for the night. Similarly, when Rocco would leave to go back to his mom's, I would express my love for him as well. Now that Bruno is in college, I continue the tradition of telling him I love him before we hang up the phone. When he visits, I always say "I love you" before Damon and I go to bed, or before Bruno leaves the house to run errands, visit friends, or see his mom in the mountains.

Involve them in acts of love. Encourage them to express their feelings through letters, drawings, or kind gestures for others. Teaching them to give and receive love strengthens their emo-tional intelligence and helps them build strong relationships in the future. You're not just loving them; you're teaching them how to love. Bruno and I have built something special: open commu-nication and trust. He knows he can come to me if something is bothering him. If he's upset with me, he can tell me respectfully, and I won't get defensive. This practice has created deep trust and a stronger emotional connection between us. That's the power of consistent, intentional love.

As a Bad-Ass Bonus Mom, you have the incredible opportunity to shape your children's lives through love. Remember, love is a language that knows no bounds. Shower them with affection, celebrate their uniqueness, show up for their moments, listen without judgment, and let them know they are cherished—today and always—because children need as much love as possible, and you have the power to give it—being the strongest anchor in their lives.

Growing Pains Are Where the Real Work Happens

I love you too. Really wish you were here. Bruno

The first time I grounded Bruno, I felt like I was failing. He'd repeatedly broken curfew after I'd warned him, setting a clear boundary: another infraction would mean losing his phone for a month. When he broke the rule, I took his phone and instantly felt like a villain. Damon wanted to negotiate, to give Bruno another chance and be the "good guy," but I couldn't. I had made a promise, and failing to follow through would render every boundary I set afterward meaningless. So I held firm, feeling like the worst person in the house. That month was brutal—not just because Bruno was angry and didn't speak to me for days, but because I had to sit with the discomfort of being the "bad guy." I officially wasn't the "fun girlfriend" anymore, if I ever truly was. I was the one actually parenting, and that didn't feel good. What I didn't expect was what happened after the first week without his phone. Bruno became more engaged, more present, and actually talked to us. He played games with the family. He was *here*. I realized something profound: he didn't need me to be fun; he needed me to be consistent. He needed to know that actions had consequences and that I cared enough to enforce them. That's a growing pain nobody tells you about. It's not just the painful moments of conflict; it's the realization that being a bonus mom sometimes means being the adult in the room, even when it costs you, even when it makes you unpopular.

With Rocco, the growing pains were different and much slower. He lived with his mom most of the time, which limited my opportunities to build a strong connection. When he came to our house, he experienced the whiplash of two completely different parenting styles. His mom did everything for him, but I expected him to learn responsibility, so he pushed back. He'd "accidentally" kick me and challenge me with endless questions. Yikes! He was testing whether I was safe, whether I was going to stay, and whether my care was genuine or just an act. It took a long time to get through that—much longer than with Bruno—because Rocco and I lacked the daily consistency that builds trust. The breakthrough didn't come through discipline or long talks; it happened underwater during a family vacation. We were playing a silly game, seeing who could hold their breath the longest, and something shifted. He realized I wasn't a threat. I was simply there, playing with him, not trying to fix him or earn his acceptance. I was simply present. After that, he started to open up. The kicking lessened, and the battles became less frequent. Now, he's one of the most incredible kids, but it took all those growing pains to get there—every moment of discomfort, uncertainty, and effort that didn't always feel productive.

Here's what nobody tells you about growing pains: they don't feel like progress; they feel like failure. You'll have moments when you question everything, wonder if this blended family thing was a mistake, or feel like you're doing everything wrong. You may feel resentment from the kids and a lack of support from your partner. Badass Bonus Moms, this is real talk. However, those moments *are* the growing pains. They do lessen in time, and they're where the real transformation happens. We're taught that relationships should feel good all the time, that if something's hard, something's wrong. That's not true! In a blended family, hard is normal. Uncomfortable is normal. Misunderstanding is normal. If you expect it to feel smooth, you'll interpret every rough patch as a sign of failure instead of a sign of growth. I had to learn that my bonus kids being resistant didn't mean they'd never accept me. It meant they were processing a lot. They were figuring out where I fit while dealing with loyalty conflicts with their mom, fear, and uncertainty. My job wasn't to make that comfortable for them; it was to stay steady through it.

This meant not taking their resistance personally, understanding that their pushback was part of their journey, not a rejection of me. I didn't demand they accept me, love me, or call me by a certain name. I simply showed up consistently while they figured things out. This process is hard, and you will fumble—and that's okay. The other growing pain nobody talks about is your own. I had to confront my triggers and realized my patience was thinner, and my flexibility less, than I believed. Instead of seeing that as failure, I saw it as an invitation to grow. This was a game changer. Every time I felt frustrated with the boys or with Damon, I had a choice: blame them for not adjusting fast enough, or examine what was coming up in me and work with that. Usually, it came down to control—wanting them to accept me before they were ready—and my own abandonment issues being triggered by their resistance. I feared investing so much time, love, and energy into kids who might never fully accept me or could be pulled out of my life if Damon and I broke up. These feelings weren't paranoia; they stemmed from genuine concern because I cared so much, and that was scary.

Here's the thing: the real growing pain isn't managing their behavior, but managing your own nervous system so you can actually show up for them. I remember directly asking Bruno, "What do you need from me?" Instead of getting defensive or trying to convince him I was good, I just listened. Sometimes, he needed space. Sometimes, it was me showing up at his lacrosse games. Sometimes, it was simply being there. The breakthrough with Rocco came when I finally stopped trying to be his bonus mom and let the relationship be what it was. I wasn't his parent or his friend. I was an adult committed to showing up consistently, even in the ambiguity and discomfort of not knowing exactly what my role was. That consistency, over time, created trust. Ladies, this is a hard concept to grasp. You are not perfect, nor are you expected to be. You may have great weeks when you think you've figured it out, only to have terrible weeks that make you feel like you're back at square one. This cycle is completely natural in blended families. Progress moves in cycles—break-through, setback, adjustment, and breakthrough—the cycle repeats. But on the other side, you build something real, not perfect, but real.

The kids didn't instantly love me; that took time. But now they trust me. They know I mean what I say, that I'll show up when they really need me. They know I'm not going anywhere just because things get uncomfortable. That trust was built through all those growing pains, through every moment I wanted to give up but didn't, through every boundary I held firm, even when it cost me something, through every conversation where I admitted

I didn't know what I was doing but was determined to figure it out anyway. As Bruno wrote in a card, "Happy Mother's Day, Michelle. Thank you for always being there for me, even when I'm challenging. Love you so much."

Being Badass Bonus Moms isn't about avoiding the growing pains. Bruno wasn't a "challenging" child; he just had challenging moments, like we all do. Being Badass Bonus Moms is about walking through those moments with your eyes open, knowing that discomfort is where real connection gets built. It's about staying present even when it doesn't feel like anything is working. It's about understanding that the messy middle is where actual family is created. And most importantly, it's about how you navigate parenting alongside a partner who's a "Disney Dad"—because that's a whole other layer to this journey.

So, Badass Bonus Moms, remember: growing pains are proof you're building something real. That something real is worth every uncomfortable moment, every tear shed, and every ounce of love you pour into this beautiful, chaotic family you're creating. Embrace the journey, trust the process, and know that every step you take brings you closer to the connections you desire.

Inhale Peace, Exhale Frustration

Happy Anniversary. You are very special to me & my boys.
Thanks for all that you do. Love Damon

Mastering the art of breathing while navigating the complexities of blended family life can feel like a circus act, juggling flaming torches on a unicycle. Some days call for a deep breath; others, a primal scream.

Smartwatches often remind us to breathe, which seems obvious until you realize you're holding your breath more often than you think. Amid the chaos of sibling squabbles, homework meltdowns, and the endless "where's my...?" moments, it's easy to forget this essential tool.

When stress rises, pause and inhale deeply through your nose. Hold the breath for a few seconds, and exhale slowly through your mouth. Repeat, or use whatever breathing technique works for you or has been recommended by your doctor. A few breaths can ground you and clear your mind.

However, breathing isn't a cure-all. Sometimes, you reach a breaking point where screaming feels necessary, and that's okay. Find a healthy outlet: a pillow, a car ride, a closet, or a closed bathroom door. We all have days when the kids push us to the edge.

Take Bruno, for instance. We've had an ongoing debate about drinking glasses. He grabs one with his meal and then leaves it out, thinking, "Why put it away when I can use it again?" My logic? "Please put your dirty glass in the dishwasher!" The more I ask, the more my patience wears thin. But I'm not facing this challenge alone. Damon has also realized the illogic of Bruno's reasoning, and we're tackling it together.

Then there's Rocco, who has a different set of challenges. His mom takes care of everything, making it hard for him to understand that he needs to clean up after himself in our home. Through patience and guidance, we've shown him the importance of responsibility. He's not perfect, but he's learning, and I've chosen to appreciate the progress.

From both experiences, I've learned that deep breaths followed by choosing your battles is crucial for survival as a badass bonus mom. Maybe it's not about glasses for you; perhaps it's something else entirely. The key is to understand why you're feeling upset, communicate your feelings clearly, and find compromises that work for everyone. Learning to let go and breathe in those frustrating moments is where real growth happens.

Try channeling that energy creatively. Instead of screaming, grab a journal or sketchbook and let the frustration flow onto the page. Write a letter to your future self about how you handled the chaos, or doodle your feelings away. This releases tension and offers a fresh perspective.

Don't underestimate the power of humor. When overwhelmed,

try to find the funny side. Imagine the scene: juice spilled, Wi-Fi down, and you contemplating your life choices. Instead of losing it, laugh! Frame it as a hilarious family moment.

I remember the first time I unleashed an F-bomb; it shocked Damon, Bruno, and especially Rocco, who cried. I felt awful. Damon came in and said with a concerned laugh, "Princess, is it safe? Have you tamed the dragon?" I started laughing through my tears. That's the bonus of having a "Disney Dad" around – he brings levity.

Laughter lightens the mood and helps everyone breathe easier.

Of course, sometimes you need to scream, and that's perfectly fine. Expressing frustration is healthy, but timing is key. If you feel the urge to scream at the kids, wait until you're alone—and not in public, if possible. Alternatively, letting out your emotions in the shower is a classic, personal sound booth. You could also channel that scream energy into action: clean, run, or tackle a DIY (do it yourself) project, like organizing drawers or cleaning out your closet. Moving your body shifts your mindset and helps you process intense feelings.

When I've wanted to scream, I've run around our neighborhood, worked out, called my sisters Tanya or Kimberly, or gone to CorePower Yoga. Re-grounding myself on my mat does wonders.

The true measure of your actions reveals itself in the most challenging moments. I'll never forget one frantic Thursday night. I arrived home to find Damon collapsed in the bathroom, burning with fever, while upstairs, Bruno and Rocco were restless, hungry for their dinner.

Amidst that whirlwind, I juggled salmon sizzling on the stove, checked Damon's fever, and tried to keep the boys calm. I projected an air of normalcy, forcing a smile as I placed plates before them, distracting them with questions about school and their lives—anything to keep their minds off the quiet moans coming from the next room.

Once the boys finished eating, I ushered them out of the kitchen so I could focus on getting Damon settled. After he finally fell asleep, I sat in the dark, quiet house, realizing I hadn't eaten.

Remember, you are the quiet force that maintains equilibrium, and that is no small feat. It is everything.

Ultimately, learning when to breathe and when to scream is essential. Embrace the chaos, find your outlets, and remember it's okay to feel overwhelmed. GIVE YOURSELF GRACE. You're doing an incredible job on this rollercoaster! Take a deep breath, laugh at the absurdity, and when the moment calls for it, let that scream out.

What emotions did it stir within you, and how did you navigate those feelings?

What lessons did you learn from this experience, and how can you apply them moving forward?

Creating the Outcome You Want

Being a Badass Bonus Mom isn't easy. It's more than just being the "fun adult" who hands out cookies and lets the kids stay up late. The real question you need to ask yourself is: "What outcome do I actually want?" Because the answer changes everything.

Let's be real. If your goal is for your bonus kids to instantly love you by saying "yes" to every request and doing everything for them, you might feel like you're on the right track. But here's the thing: that path leads straight to chaos and resentment for everyone involved. I've seen it happen too often: divorced parents get caught in a competition of who can say "yes" the loudest. Gifts, trips, fancy experiences—it can turn into a battle for brownie points that's exhausting and ultimately fruitless. That's not parenting; that's buying affection, and spoiler alert: it doesn't work. My partner loves his two boys fiercely but sometimes thinks doing everything for them is the ultimate expression of love. I can relate; I'm a giver, too. There's real joy in making someone's day better. But here's the thing: when you're the only one putting in the effort, it's not love—it's a one-way street, and trust me, those streets are draining.

Let me share a bit of my backstory. I grew up in a home where chores were non-negotiable. Washing dishes, cleaning rooms, doing laundry, and cooking were all part of learning to survive. They weren't punishments; they were life skills. So, when I found a partner raised in the same environment, I thought I had it all figured out. Plot twist: that training didn't magically transfer to his kids.

When we moved into my tiny one-bedroom condo—me, Damon, and his two boys—I quickly understood the challenges ahead. Then COVID hit, shrinking our space even further and highlighting the extent of the work I faced. These kids had never washed a dish or made their beds, and the bathroom? The toilet seat was perpetually up, with no attempt to clean. Laundry was another foreign concept; they'd never done it. I know what you're thinking: his boys grew up with a weekly maid and parents who didn't expect much. That's essentially it. Here's the twist: my partner's own mother taught him chores as a child. So, where did those lessons go when he became a dad? That's when I realized something crucial: you must set clear, honest boundaries about what you're willing to do—and what you absolutely won't. Otherwise, you'll find yourself drowning in draining situations. The biggest challenge? Your partner expecting you to fill the role his ex-wife played. If that doesn't sit right, shut it down immediately. Your sanity depends on it.

Kids will test the waters when it comes to how they can talk to and treat you because you're not their biological mom. Address it when you see it happening. They may push back, but they ultimately respect boundaries. They need to understand that you're an adult in the same house who deserves basic respect. That's not mean; it's reality. Choose your battles wisely; don't nitpick everything—that helps no one. You'll have learning curves, and you'll figure out what works as you go. But the truth is, saying "yes" to everything isn't parenting; it's a disservice. When kids never hear "no," they can become spoiled and entitled—essentially unpleasant. That's not fair to them or you. The tone you use matters more than you realize; kids sense uncertainty and hesitation immediately. Respect isn't given; it's earned with time and by setting boundaries, holding them accountable, and following through. I've learned that every action—good or bad—has consequences. So ask yourself: do you want your partner's kids prepared for the world when they leave home? If the answer is yes, it's time to step into this role and do the work.

Ladies, setting a boundary doesn't guarantee instant results. Kids are natural experimenters, constantly testing limits. They'll push to see how far they can go before you crack. This is where staying steady matters. Stand firm. If you say, "No hanging out until your homework is done," don't waver. The moment you backtrack, you undermine your word—and that's not the foundation you want to build.

Want the kids to help around the house? Be specific about what that means. Create a chore chart—I love these! Better yet, make it a game. Turn cleanup into a family competition to see who can tidy their room fastest. You'd be amazed how much kids step up when it's fun, not punishment. In our home, Saturdays are chore days. Each boy has specific tasks to tackle, and Damon and I pitch in. To make our chore day enjoyable, Damon plays music throughout the house, creating a lively atmosphere as we clean.

This is where his "Disney dad" side shines. He walks around with a positive attitude, encouraging the boys with comments like, "Won't you be happy to enjoy a clean room?" or "Can't you wait to shower in your sparkling bathroom?" His enthusiasm makes it feel less like a chore and more like a fun family activity.

Share your own childhood stories. Show them everyone contributes—not to cause suffering, but because that's how families function. It's about teamwork and creating a home everyone enjoys and is proud of. I've openly shared my upbringing with Bruno and Rocco, detailing our chores and my parents' expectations. With both my parents working full-time—until my mom attended law school while my dad traveled frequently—my siblings and I had significant responsibilities. I've shared my own stresses and struggles, including feeling like an outsider or facing dark thoughts. I often got grounded, which helps me relate to their feelings. These vulnerable moments matter. They show Bruno and Rocco that I'm not just giving them chores for the sake of it; there's a deeper reason behind my guidance. By sharing my experiences, I hope to help them understand the value of responsibility and the positive outcomes of family teamwork. It's about fostering resilience and creating a supportive environment where we can all learn and grow.

But here's where the real magic happens: when you set firm boundaries and stick to them, teaching that actions have consequences and that respect matters. That's when things shift. The kids start to understand that you're serious, that you care enough not to let them become entitled, and that you're genuinely invested in who they become. One day—maybe not tomorrow, maybe not for years—they'll thank you. They might not realize it now, but you're not just shaping their childhood.

Badass Bonus Moms, you're equipping them for life. You're

teaching them skills and values they'll need as adults. You're showing them what real love looks like: not always easy or fun, but consistent, firm, and genuinely invested in their growth. So step into your power. Set those boundaries, hold your ground, and know that you're not just a bonus mom—you're a vital force shaping the future. Your commitment to their development will pay off in ways you can't even imagine. Keep shining!

Identifying Your Needs Through "No"

Michelle, I hope that you have an amazing Birthday. Sorry if I have been difficult lately, just know that I love you and am very grateful for all you have and are doing/have done. Love, Bruno

Why are we taught on airplanes to put on our own oxygen masks first, before helping children? Yet, we often allow our bonus kids, our partners, the very family we are creating, to drain our energy as if we were tireless robots. Ouch! Why do we feel guilty about prioritizing our own needs, or expressing that we need a break? For far too long, I immersed myself in the endless cycle of cooking, grocery shopping, managing schedules, creating chore lists, and establishing rules, all while balancing my own career. I wore many hats: disciplinarian, cheerleader, and the often unseen laborer of being a Badass Bonus Mom.

Amid this whirlwind of responsibilities, I began to feel the weight of my unrecognized efforts. I had been saying "yes" so often that I lost sight of my own needs, becoming invisible in the process. I love Bruno, Rocco, and Damon, but I felt like I was disappearing—managing everything without anyone checking in or acknowledging my contributions. The truth was, I never voiced my feelings until I reached a breaking point. One night, I found myself collapsed in my closet, exhausted and empty. I realized that if I didn't express my needs, no one would magically know them.

Taking a deep breath, I initiated a courageous conversation with Damon. "I need to talk," I began, "because I'm not okay." I laid everything bare: how I sometimes felt like a babysitter rather than a partner, how I was suffocating under the weight of invisible labor, and how desperately I needed to be seen—not just for what I did for his kids, but for who I was as an individual. I craved time for myself and a more equitable division of responsibilities.

Here's the thing, ladies: as Badass Bonus Moms, we often convince ourselves, consciously or unconsciously, that we can take on this role because we are superheroes, swooping in to save the day—to fix anything emotionally or mentally that affected the family before we arrived. We try hard not to complain, because we don't want our partners to think their kids aren't important to us. We put ourselves on the back burner, ready to be needed when they are sick, available for their activities, or perhaps just to wind us up and have us dance around like monkeys. (Okay, maybe not that last one, but sometimes it can feel that way!) Stop! Your sanity and health cannot sustain this. I know, because I've experienced more health issues since becoming a bonus mom than in my entire life before.

Don't get me wrong. Being a bonus mom doesn't automatically lead to sickness, but it can if you don't learn to say "no" when you're tired and let go of the guilt that often accompanies it. You might have easily done this prior to becoming a bonus mom, but now you worry your bonus children will feel uncared for. Remember, caring for yourself is how you can give more to others.

To my surprise, Damon hadn't realized how overwhelmed I felt. That conversation didn't magically solve all our problems, but it opened the door to meaningful change. I discovered that clearly communicating my needs isn't selfish; it's essential. Resentment only creates distance in relationships, and I couldn't expect anyone to read my mind.

Next, I needed to identify my true needs—what would genuinely help me feel whole. I craved time alone, sincere check-ins from Damon, and recognition for my efforts. I needed to establish boundaries around work and family time.

Once I understood my needs, I communicated them directly. I told Damon, "I need one night a week just for us—no kids." I requested that he "step in more with parenting" and expressed that "I need to hear you acknowledge all that I do." Some conversations were tough and emotional, but each one mattered.

Surprisingly, as I began to articulate my needs, the kids started doing the same. They observed me setting boundaries and learned that expressing needs is healthy, not something to hide. They began asking for what they wanted instead of sulking, embracing the power of open communication.

I also learned to distinguish between needs and demands. A need is essential for well-being—like time to recharge—while a demand tends to be about control and often isn't effective.

Mastering the art of saying "no" was crucial. I practiced straightforward phrases like, "I can't do that this weekend," or "I need you to handle this." As someone who naturally wants to care for Bruno, Rocco, and Damon, this was a challenge. However, I soon discovered that saying "no" to what drained me created space to say "yes" to what truly matters.

There were times when Damon invited me to join him and the boys for a bike ride—usually to grab lunch or ice cream. If I was too tired, I would thank him for the invite but suggest they enjoy that time together. I explained that I was too drained and didn't want to pretend to have a good time. Initially, Bruno would plead, "Please, Michele, come!" While that felt flattering, standing my ground felt even better. I realized I didn't need to always be present; I already spent quality time with them when Damon was away.

I also recognized that my needs would evolve over time. What I required in the early days of being a bonus mom was different from what I needed as our family dynamic changed. Life is fluid, and so are our needs. The most remarkable shift? Once I began voicing my needs, the resentment faded away.

Now, when the boys want to play basketball at the park, I see it as another opportunity for them to bond with their dad. I even encourage Damon to take the boys skiing every year since they love it, and I prefer to sit those outings out. Although this hasn't happened yet, Damon knows I'm supportive because having time apart makes our reunions even sweeter.

I still work hard and show up, but now it's from a place of choice, not obligation. I do it because I want to, not because I feel I have to earn my place in this family. Being a Badass Bonus Mom doesn't mean losing ourselves in the role; it means showing up as our full selves—complete with our needs and boundaries.

Your family can't meet needs they don't know about, and your partner can't support you if you're silently struggling. Your kids won't learn healthy communication if you don't model it. So, be clear, be direct, and be honest about what you need. Stand firm in that truth.

You are not asking for too much; you are claiming what you deserve—a place at the table as a whole person, not just as the one managing everything. Embrace the power of saying "no" as a way of saying "yes" to yourself and your well-being. It's time to prioritize your needs and create a harmonious family dynamic that empowers everyone involved.

Relationship Priority

*Princess, I miss you when you're not a part of my daily life.
I feel like we're stronger than ever, and the next chapter
will be amazing. Now, back to the issue at hand:
Let's get a room!
Love, Damon*

I'm about to say something that might be controversial in the blended family world: your relationship with your partner is the foundation of everything. I can sense some of you bristling, but this is absolutely important; IT TRULY IS THE FOUNDATION OF EVERYTHING.

When stepping into the role of a Bad-Ass Bonus Mom, it's easy to get wrapped up in parenting and put your relationship with your partner on the back burner. You find yourself managing kids' schedules, navigating co-parenting dynamics, establishing boundaries, and creating traditions—suddenly, your partner feels like a roommate you occasionally have sex with, whom you happen to love. And that's not just sad—it's dangerous.

The strongest foundation your blended family can have is a

connected partnership. Kids need to see a genuine, loving relationship, especially those whose parents' relationships fell apart. Research confirms that when the couple's relationship is strong and prioritized, children feel more secure.

Let's keep it real: when you connect intimately with your partner, it triggers physiological changes that reduce stress and help you let go of frustrations that don't serve you or your family. Regular, intentional intimacy makes you calmer, more patient, and less likely to sweat the small stuff or hold onto grudges about who forgot to take out the trash. Whenever I find myself getting agitated with Damon, I reflect on the last time we were sexually intimate, and it all clicks into place.

Damon and I share a strong sexual connection, but with our demanding schedules and my role as a bonus mom, intimacy can easily fall by the wayside. Since Bruno started college, those moments have become more frequent, but they can still be elusive. The instant we reconnect physically, it feels like a reset button. Suddenly, the things that might have annoyed me—or vice versa—transform into cute and funny quirks.

Here's the thing: when you immerse yourself in being a bonus mom, it's easy to forget about your partner and the love that brought you together in the first place. Those feelings of excitement can morph into frustration, nagging, and nitpicking.

It's easy to become so focused on parenting that you lose sight of your partnership, and suddenly question why you chose this person. Maintaining a strong relationship is as vital as nurturing your bond with your bonus kids; without that solid foundation, everything else can crumble. Romantic connection isn't a luxury; it's essential. While expressing your love physically, verbally is also important, acting on it reinforces your bond. Words without action are simply unfulfilled promises. Your partner needs to *feel* prioritized, not just be told they are, and you deserve to feel that too; you deserve to be loved well.

Stephanie, Happy Valentine's Day. You make every day spaecial. Thanks for being my everything. Love Damon

Ladies, there is always time for connection—you just have to intentionally protect those moments. Perhaps you wake up early to share coffee before the day's chaos begins, watch the sunrise together in silence, or schedule a non-negotiable date night. It could be sitting close on the couch during a movie while the kids watch from across the room, cooking dinner together while flirting, or simply offering a long embrace when your partner comes home instead of immediately launching into logistics.

When Damon and I met on July 13th, we consciously decided to celebrate our relationship every month. On the 13th, we do something special to acknowledge why we chose each other. This tradition helps us navigate challenges and keeps us tethered when life feels chaotic. Some months it's simple: sharing coffee at our favorite café, enjoying music by our fire pit, or taking a hand-in-hand stroll around the neighborhood, sharing five things we appreciate about each other. Other times, it's lunch together or a deliberate date night we call "ST"—sexy time. This is how we model what a partnership should look like. This tradition may sound simple, but it's been revolutionary for us. It reminds us that we choose each other every day, not out of obligation, but because we genuinely want to. That choice allows us to be better parents.

Happy Anniversary, Another wonderful month, You make me so very happy. It's amazing that we found each other. Love Damon.

When Bruno tests boundaries or Rocco struggles with communication, Damon and I can look at each other and remember: we're a team. We chose this, we choose each other. Children are always watching. They absorb how you treat one another, how you recover from disagreements, and how you show affection. They learn what a relationship looks like by observing yours. When they see you hug, share a glass of wine, or exchange loving words, you're creating a safe environment that is priceless, especially for children of divorced parents. They need to see that love can work, commitment is real, and two people can choose each other and build something beautiful together.

We look forward to the 13th of each month, our personal anniversary, as a special day to celebrate Damon and our relationship. I also cherish Father's Day, his birthdays, and even Hallmark holidays—any occasion that prompts me to express my love for him. Finding the perfect card, writing heartfelt messages, and choosing gifts that reflect my love and appreciation bring me joy, especially knowing he will feel that love each time he sees, uses, or remembers them. Spending Christmas and New Year's together is also important, as it reminds us of our ability to face anything together and allows us to celebrate the possibilities of the coming year. When I travel for more than a week, I leave behind a card or small gift as a reminder that he's always in my thoughts, even when I'm away. We also make it a point to connect daily, ensuring our communication remains consistent. These are the things that keep us prioritizing each other and our relationship.

Of course, we've also had important conversations and been open about our needs. Romance, intimacy, and even simple expressions of love can easily fade without intentional communication, even if the feelings are still there. The same goes for needing more support from your partner, especially when navigating the challenges of being a bonus mom—ask for what you need! Men aren't mind readers—although we all wish they were, so vocalize your needs instead of making assumptions.

Let's be clear, prioritizing your partner is a two-way street. Being Badass Bonus Moms doesn't mean we should bear the brunt of parenting, household management, and maintaining our emotional connection alone. That's not a partnership—that's a recipe for exhaustion and resentment. Your partner must show up, too. They need to remember why they chose you: open doors, initiate conversations, and plan dates. They have to make time and want this as much as you do. So, have that conversation. Be clear about your needs. Tell your partner that you're not interested in being co-parenting roommates—you want a real relationship. You need to feel chosen. The kids need to see two people who genuinely love each other and make time for one another. When you prioritize your partnership, everything shifts. Stress decreases, laughter increases, and the kids feel more secure witnessing what commitment truly looks like. They see that love requires effort, choice, and intentionality. Remember why you're doing this: you're not just a bonus mom managing chaos. You're also a partner—a woman deserving of love, con-nection, and intimacy. So, wake up early for coffee. Schedule date nights and protect them fiercely. Hold hands during walks. Exchange anniversary cards.

Princes, Happy 6 Year Anniversary!
Crazy how fast time has gone by...
Amazing memories and more to come.
Thanks for being my partner in life.
Love Damon

Make time for intimate connections—multiple times a month, if possible. Look at your partner as the one who matters most, because they should. Model what real partnership looks like for your bonus kids, and remind them—as well as yourself—that you didn't choose this blended family life just to parent; you chose it because you chose them. That's what being Badass Bonus Moms is all about: building a life filled with love, laughter, and resilience, where every moment spent together strengthens the bonds that truly matter.

Show Up First

Stephanie, Glad you're back to watch movies. Love, Rocco

The first time Bruno rolled his eyes at me, I took it personally. I had consistently shown up, been kind (though sterner than his dad), and been reliable. Yet, he treated me like an inconvenience. I remember thinking, *I deserve better than this. I'm trying so hard, and he won't even give me a chance.*

Then, I realized something: he didn't owe me respect simply for being present. Respect isn't an entitlement earned by effort; it's built through consistent actions, and he had no reason to trust me yet. I had to learn the difference between expecting respect and earning it. To be clear, though, all children should show a basic level of respect to adults, period.

I learned at a young age that a basic tenet of respect was to never speak disrespectfully to any adult—parents, grandparents, neighbors, etc. "Yes, Ma'am" and "No, Sir" were simply expected. This didn't mean that I couldn't speak up if I felt unsafe or uncomfortable; it simply meant that the way I spoke to my friends was unacceptable when addressing an adult.

For the first year, I thought if I could just prove myself—show him I was trustworthy, reliable, and fun—he'd automatically respect me. When he started playing lacrosse, I showed up to most of his games. I remembered his preferences. I was present and engaged, trying so hard to be someone he could count on. And he still rolled his eyes.

The turning point came when I stopped trying to be his parent and started being honest about who I was. When Bruno first lived with us, I realized that he had his own narrative about me: I was the woman in his dad's life, the intruder, the one stealing his dad's attention. He didn't *have* to respect me; he had every reason to resent me.

Instead of pushing for his respect, I started respecting him. I recognized that he was dealing with a lot, and I acknowledged that his feelings about me were complicated and valid. I respected that he didn't have to like or accept me, and I stopped taking his resistance personally.

Then something shifted. When I stopped demanding his respect, he started offering it. It began with small moments: he'd mention something that happened at school and actually wait for my response; he'd ask me a question about something I cared about; he'd laugh at a joke I made. These tiny moments showed him deciding, on his own, that maybe I was worth a little respect. I knew I had to follow through.

I always kept my promises. I wouldn't promise to be at his game and then flake; if I couldn't be there, I wouldn't commit. Each time I showed up—not just physically, but emotionally—I built respect. The same principle applied with Rocco: he needed to learn that I meant what I said. When I told him something, I followed through. When I set a boundary, I held it. When I said I'd listen, I listened instead of scrolling through my phone.

That consistency built respect. However, there's a less-discussed aspect: I also had to respect myself enough to demand respect in return.

There were times when Bruno spoke to me dismissively. The first time, mostly out of shock, I let it slide. I thought, "He's a kid dealing with a lot. I can take it." But that taught him it was okay to treat me poorly. So one day, I sat him down and said, "I understand this situation is difficult for you, and that you didn't ask for me to be here. However, I deserve basic courtesy, and if you can't provide that, we're going to have a problem." He got defensive and pushed back, but I held the line. Interestingly, he started respecting me *more*, not less, because I'd finally shown him I had standards and wouldn't accept whatever he threw at me. That respect was reciprocal. I had to do the same with Damon. There were moments when he'd make decisions affecting me without asking for my input, or side with the boys without hearing my perspective. Initially, I let it go, not wanting to seem difficult or unsupportive, but that taught him my opinion didn't matter. So I started speaking up: "I need you to ask me before you make decisions that affect me. I need you to hear my perspective." When he did, he showed me respect in return.

Ladies, when you step into the role of Badass Bonus Moms, remember that respect isn't about being liked; it's about being valued. It's about everyone in the family understanding that each person's needs and feelings matter. It's about following through on promises and maintaining boundaries. To keep it real, this also looks different with different people.

Bruno needed me to respect his independence and his right to feel however he felt about me being there. Rocco needed me to be reliable and playful. Damon needed me to advocate for myself so he knew I had standards. When I started *really* respecting them—not just performing it—they started respecting me back. Not because I'd earned some magical status, but because I'd shown them what respect looked like, modeled it, demanded it when it wasn't given, and maintained it consistently over time. As you navigate your role as a Bad-Ass Bonus Mom, remember that showing up is just the beginning; it's the foundation on which deeper relationships are built.

Every moment you invest in understanding your bonus kids, every boundary you set, and every time you advocate for yourself is a step toward forging a genuine connection. You are not just a caregiver but a vital part of their story, and you have the power to shape that narrative. Each act of respect you extend teaches them the value of respect in return, showing them that love isn't just about feelings but about actions. So, as you embrace this journey, take pride in the moments that may seem small but are profoundly impactful. Celebrate the victories—no matter how minor—because they are the threads that weave your family together. And when the road gets tough or respect feels hard to earn, remember that you are building a legacy. You're not just a bonus mom; you are a foundational pillar in their lives. Your presence and commitment matter, and they will see that over time. Continue to show up, continue to respect, and watch as the relationships you nurture transform into something beautiful and lasting. You are Badass Bonus Moms, and your journey is just beginning.

Bonding Moments

Happy Birthday Michelle! I am so grateful for all you have done for me and that you came into my life when you did. I appreciate all the advice and input you have on my life and will always love you. Love Bruno

Badass Bonus Moms, here's something that doesn't make it into parenting books or perfectly lit Instagram posts: bonding moments. I'm not talking about forced family game nights where everyone smiles through gritted teeth or planned vacations where you're trying so hard to create memories that nobody actually enjoys. I'm talking about the real moments—the ones that sneak up on you, the ones that become *your* thing.

When Bruno first called me "Michelle," I literally tilted my head, wondering, *Why Michelle?* My first name is Stephanie. Shouldn't he call me that? So I asked him, and he said, "My mom has a few friends named Stephanie, so I want to call you by your middle name—Michelle. Plus, Michelle is a cool name." This name change was that simple for him.

In that moment, something shifted. My heart fluttered with

so much love and joy that I almost didn't know what to do with it. He not only remembered my middle name from the one time I told him, but he also didn't *have* to use it. He could have called me Stephanie like everyone else. But he chose to make me different. He chose to make me feel special by using my middle name. And now? That's *our* thing—the thing that belongs only to him and me. Every time he calls me Michelle, it's like a little bonus-son love note.

Damon loves to call me "Princess" or "Bae" (I also call him "Bae"), and we love celebrating the 13th of every month as a reminder of why we wake up and choose each other every day.

Here's the thing: bonding doesn't happen because you plan it. It happens because you're willing to let your bonus kids create their own identity with you—when they feel safe enough to make you something special, something that's just theirs.

Now, ladies, not all bonding moments happen naturally or easily. Some bonus moms and bonus kids have to work for it. Some relationships take years to develop real affection, and that's okay. You're not failing if you don't have a magical connection with your bonus kids right away. You're human, and so are they. Sometimes it just takes time.

The key is intention: showing up, paying attention, noticing when they do something special, and celebrating it. It's about creating traditions that acknowledge both your role as a bonus parent and the reality of their biological parent.

My friend Kimberly and her bonus daughter Laila have a beautiful tradition that perfectly illustrates this. Every year on Mother's Day, they get matching bracelets—not out of obligation or some grand plan, but because Kimberly saw an opportunity to create something special, and Laila was happy to participate. It's their thing—a bonding moment that says, "I celebrate us."

Similarly, on Laila's birthday, Kimberly makes it a Kimberly-and-Laila day. She doesn't try to replace Laila's biological mom; instead, depending on custody schedules, they celebrate before, on, or after the actual birthday—whatever works—jetting off together to create their own memories.

This is the kind of bonding that truly works in blended families. It's not about being the favorite but about creating your own unique relationship. Bonding moments aren't always big or planned. Sometimes, it's simply sitting with your bonus kid while they cry about something unrelated to you. Other times, it's remembering they hate pickles and making sure their plate is pickle-free. Or it could be laughing together over something silly—and for a moment, you're just two people connecting. Bonding moments are the inside jokes nobody else understands, the knowing look across the dinner table that sparks shared laughter, the moment your bonus kid seeks your advice instead of their biological parent, and the times they let their guard down around you, even slightly.

Sometimes, bonding is hard-earned. You might spend months—or even years—trying to connect before something finally clicks. It can be exhausting to feel like you're always the one making the effort. But then, one day, something shifts. Maybe they finally trust you enough to be real, realize you're not going anywhere, or see that you genuinely care, not out of obligation, but because you want to.

Some bonding moments come from shared struggle. When you go through something difficult together—a conflict at school, a family crisis—you're suddenly on the same team, no longer opponents but allies. That's when real connection happens. It's important to understand that bonding doesn't have to resemble what you see on Pinterest or social media. It doesn't have to be picture-perfect or happen on some prescribed timeline. Bonding is messy, real, and sometimes awkward; it can even take years. But when it happens—when your bonus kid does something that shows they see you as "their" person—that's magic.

I love watching movies with Rocco; it's our bonding moment. He's always open to my suggestions, even if it's not something he would typically watch. He stays awake, pays attention, and talks about it with me. He's also introduced me to so many great movies and TV series.

Pay attention to those moments—the ones where they choose you, create an inside joke, or carve out a space that's just for you two. Notice when they let their guard down, when they trust you with something real, when they're willing to be vulnerable around you. These bonding moments don't require a big budget or lots of planning; they require presence. They require you to show up consistently, be genuinely interested in who they are, and be willing to let them create their own relationship with you instead of forcing one. Bruno calling me Michelle and the handshake he created for us? That's his way of saying, "You matter to me enough to be different from anyone else." Kimberly and Laila's matching bracelets? That's their way of saying, "We have something special." All of us with our inside jokes, nicknames, and traditions? That's our way of saying, "We're a family, and we do things our own way." Don't underestimate the power of these moments. They're not big or flashy, but they're everything. They're proof that you're building something real, that your bonus kids can love you—not as a replacement for their biological parent but as someone unique and special in their lives. They're proof that blended families can actually work.

Create space for bonding and intentionally notice when it occurs. Celebrate it. Hold onto it. Most importantly, allow your bonus kids to define your relationship instead of forcing it into a predetermined shape. The best bonding moments in blended families are the unique ones that make you smile, the ones that say, "This person chose me, and I chose them, and together we created something that's just ours." As you continue this journey, remember that each bonding moment is a thread woven into the rich tapestry of your family. These connections, no matter how small or seemingly insignificant, are the fabric of love that holds you together. They remind you that you are not just filling a role; you are building a life filled with shared laughter, inside jokes, and unconditional support. Embrace the chaos, cherish the quirks, and let the beauty of these moments inspire you to forge ahead. You are crafting a uniquely personal narrative, and that is the true magic of being a Badass Bonus Mom.

You Can't Pour From an Empty Cup

Princess is back in town. I truly miss you when we are not together, although I know you need your time by the beach. Love, Damon.

I used to think self-care was a luxury reserved for people without kids, a distant concept for someone trying to prove her worth in a blended family—something I often did before becoming a bonus mom. Each morning, I woke up early, determined to get ahead of the chaos. I skipped lunch to tackle countless tasks and canceled plans with friends because someone always needed something. My own needs fell to the bottom of the list—below everyone else's, household chores, and even things that didn't truly matter. I told myself this was love, that sacrificing my well-being was the hallmark of a good bonus mom. I believed that if I worked hard enough, gave enough, and immersed myself in the role, I would eventually earn the right to take care of myself. I was wrong. The turning point came on a seemingly ordinary

Tuesday when I looked in the mirror and didn't recognize the person staring back.

Ladies, it wasn't that I looked different; it was that I had become invisible. I was so busy caring for everyone else that I had completely erased myself. I couldn't remember the last time I did something just for me or what I even enjoyed anymore. I had been running on fumes for so long that fumes felt normal. That day, I sat down and realized that if I didn't change this, I would burn out and be no good to anyone—not to Damon, not to the boys, and certainly not to myself. So, I started small. I learned to say no—not just think it, but actually say it—giving myself permission to decline commitments that didn't serve me.

I began reincorporating self-care. I returned to yoga, something I loved and practiced regularly before Damon and the boys came into my life. I scheduled classes like appointments, treating them as non-negotiable. Three times a week, I found myself on the mat, and with each session, I began to feel like myself again.

Here's what I discovered: taking care of yourself isn't selfish; it's essential. When you're running on empty, everyone suffers. You might snap at the kids, resent your partner, or feel emotionally drained. But when you prioritize your well-being, you create space for joy, patience, and connection. I won't lie; the guilt was real. At first, I felt guilty for taking time for yoga and for saying no. I felt guilty for wanting time alone. That guilt echoed the lessons I had learned: that self-care was somehow wrong. But I had to face a truth: the kids didn't need a martyr as a bonus mom; they needed a Badass Bonus Mom who was whole and happy. Damon didn't need a partner who faded into the background; he needed someone who was fully present. So, I kept going.

I treated myself to more regular manicures, enjoyed coffee or brunch with friends, and allowed myself to fully engage without cutting it short out of guilt. I even took weekend trips to visit Kimberly or my mom without apologizing. And you know what happened? Everyone thrived. The house didn't fall apart in my absence.

Damon stepped up, and the boys learned to entertain themselves. I returned from my time away genuinely excited to see them, rather than just feeling functional. The truth about self-care that isn't often discussed is that it isn't just about bubble baths and face masks—though those are nice too. It's about recognizing that your life matters enough to protect it. It's about refusing to disappear into any role, no matter how noble. It's about grasping the simple fact that you can't pour from an empty cup—and that's not just poetic; it's practical wisdom. By modeling this for the boys, I showed them that taking care of yourself is not only okay, but essential. Having needs isn't a weakness; saying no is powerful. Loving your family and loving yourself are not in opposition; they actually support one another.

Princess, Happy Birthday my love. Every year has been better than the last. I am looking forward to spending all the years in your heart & life.
Love Damon

Once everyone realized I wasn't going anywhere, the entire dynamic shifted. I became a better bonus mom because I was finally taking care of myself. Yes, the guilt still lingers at times, and I sometimes question whether I'm being selfish when I take time for myself. But now I recognize that guilt for what it is—old programming—and I push back against it. I deserve a life of my own, filled with joy and fulfillment beyond managing everyone else's needs. Being Badass Bonus Moms means caring for yourself as if you matter—because you do. Your well-being isn't a luxury; it's the foundation for everything else. So keep that therapy appointment. Join that yoga class. Indulge in a bubble bath. Take that weekend getaway. Take whatever you need. Not eventually. Not when things calm down. Not when you've done enough to earn it. Take it now.

You Need Your Person

I hope that you enjoyed your trip to see your mom.
I'm glad you got the chance to do that.
I am happy to see you home again and have missed you.
I love you very much, Michelle.
Love, Bruno

Ladies, finding a safe person to confide in is essential. As badass as you are, there will be times—more often than you might think—when you simply need to express your feelings. The whirlwind of blended family life can be overwhelming, and bottling everything up can lead to an explosion (yes, even the occasional f-bomb!). Finding a safe person to share your thoughts with isn't just a luxury; it's a necessity. You need a sounding board—someone who understands, listens without judgment, and helps you sort through the chaos.

Let's keep it real: not everyone can handle your feelings. Some friends may mean well but offer advice that feels more judgmental than supportive. What you truly need is empathy and validation. Whether it's a close friend, a family member, or even a therapist, having someone who can listen without trying to "fix" everything can make all the difference.

My best friend, Kimberly, is that person for me. We've known each other for nearly two decades, and our journeys into bonus mom life aligned just a few years after mine began. Kimberly is my safe space; I can share anything with her. She offers understanding, sound advice, and unwavering support when I need it most. She gets it because she's living it, too.

Finding your safe person is about trust and empathy. You need someone who respects your feelings and understands the complexities of blended family dynamics. It's not just about sharing your day; it's about expressing your frustrations, fears, and hopes. You want to feel understood, not judged.

Be discerning about whom you choose to confide in. It's perfectly okay to set boundaries around who hears your struggles. If someone consistently dismisses your feelings or redirects the conversation back to themselves, they may not be the right fit for you. Remember, you deserve to have your feelings validated.

There have been times when I felt like throwing in the towel—not ending my relationship with Damon, but stepping back from the emotional drain that sometimes accompanied my role. I was giving too much without setting clear expectations. Parenting responsibilities seemed to fall squarely on my shoulders, and I couldn't remain a bystander. Fortunately, Kimberly understood, as she navigated similar challenges within her own blended family. And here's a little secret: it's perfectly okay to vent about the small stuff. These minor annoyances can accumulate and become significant stressors. Whether it's the kids bickering or your partner forgetting the trash, sharing these moments can lighten your load. Finding someone who can laugh with you about everyday frustrations is a breath of fresh air.

I'm also blessed to have my sister and bestie, D'Vorah, who is one of my best friends and my biggest cheerleader, even though she doesn't have children. Her perspective is refreshing; she has a knack for seeing things from angles I might miss, often helping me find clarity amidst the chaos. Sometimes, a fresh viewpoint can shift your entire mindset and recharge your energy. I remember feeling down about my role as a bonus mom and calling D'Vorah, questioning everything. She immediately said, "Those boys really love you. I see it in their faces every time I visit, and they're lucky to have you in their lives." Her perspective, coming from someone I trust deeply, gave me the strength to keep going, and I'm so glad it did.

Don't overlook the power of community. Online groups, local meet-ups, or parenting classes can connect you with other women who share your experiences. Engaging with others who understand the unique challenges of blended families can be a game-changer; it's comforting to know you're not alone.

I'm also incredibly lucky to have my sister, Tanya, who is not only my person but also a mother to two of my nieces and three of my nephews, and a bonus mom herself. We've always created a safe space for one another, and she consistently offers sound advice.

When you find that safe space to vent, make the most of it. Schedule regular check-ins—whether it's a coffee date, a phone call, FaceTime, or a walk in the park. These moments become lifelines amidst the chaos, recharging your emotional batteries and providing clarity to tackle future challenges. While venting is vital, balance it with gratitude. Don't forget to share the positive moments, too, and celebrate the small wins—whether it's a good day with the kids or a meaningful conversation with your partner. This balance helps you stay grounded and reminds you of the love that exists amidst the chaos.

During one of my visits to Kimberly in California, we were both struggling early on in our bonus mom journeys. We spent a day and night venting, but the next day, we decided to speak only positively about our new family dynamics. This shift was a game-changer, reigniting our appreciation by focusing on what made us happy. Seeking support is a sign of wisdom, not weakness; you're not meant to navigate this journey alone. Finding a safe person to confide in is crucial for self-care, nurturing your emotional health, and equipping you to handle family life's ups and downs. Ladies, you are Badass Bonus Moms, and you deserve to be heard. When life feels overwhelming, seek out that safe space, embrace the power of connection, and don't hesitate to share both your struggles and victories. You've got this, and you're not alone.

The United Front

Feeling like the villain in your own home is never fun. Bruno had broken curfew for the third time in two weeks. We'd agreed that the consequence would be losing his phone for a month—no negotiations. So, when he waltzed in an hour late, I took his phone. He was furious, of course. But the real gut punch came later that night when I overheard Damon whispering to him in the hallway, "Don't worry, I'll talk to her. We'll get it back for you in a couple of days." In that moment, I wasn't his partner; I was the obstacle, the warden. And Damon wasn't a co-parent; he was Bruno's co-conspirator. If this sounds familiar, you know that sickening feeling when an agreement evaporates because your partner can't bear to see his child disappointed.

Here's what happens when you don't present a united front: the kids stop thriving and start manipulating. They learn to play you and your partner against each other. They lose respect for both of you. And they never feel safe because the rules change depending on which parent they approach. After the phone incident, I felt defeated. I knew that if we didn't fix this, our family wouldn't survive. That weekend, I told Damon we needed to talk—just us, no kids, no phones. I didn't start by accusing him, but by expressing how his actions made me feel: "When we agree on a consequence and you go behind my back to undo it, it makes me feel like my opinion doesn't matter, like I'm just the live-in nanny, not your partner. And it sets me up to be the bad guy with your kids." He heard me—really heard me. From there, we had the most boring, unsexy, and absolutely critical conversation of our lives. We didn't just talk about rules; we talked about values. What did we want to teach these kids about responsibility, respect, and consequences? We made a list of non-negotiables: bedtimes, screen time limits, homework before play, chores. We agreed on exact consequences for breaking these rules. We wrote it all down. However, Damon still had a hard time honoring our agreements. Ugh!

Since I took on the majority of parenting responsibilities, Damon's go-to response to Bruno—if he wanted to hang out with his friends, play PS4, go to a concert or after-school activity, have friends over, or watch sports before finishing his home-work—became, "Did you ask Stephanie?" Seriously?! At first, this bothered me; I couldn't understand why he wasn't able to make decisions or deliver consequences. But then I realized this was his way of showing the boys that he trusted me, that I was significant in their lives, and that we were genuinely a team with individual strengths. Is Damon perfect? No. Neither am I. Does he still slip up? Of course. His Disney Dad instincts are deeply ingrained. But he has come a long way over the years—slowly but surely.

Here's what happened when we finally created a plan that worked for us: Bruno stopped testing boundaries because he knew they were firm. The household became calmer. My relationship with Bruno improved because he felt secure. We stopped being adversaries and started being what we were always meant to be: a team.

This requires uncomfortable conversations. You're asking your partner to choose the long-term health of his family over the short-term satisfaction of making his kid happy. You're asking him to be a parent, not just a friend. And most importantly, if he's asking you to make the hard decisions, he needs to have your back.

As you navigate this new family dynamic, remember that being a Badass Bonus Mom means being part of a united front. Collaboration and communication are key to building a foundation where everyone feels heard, valued, and secure. Your willingness to engage in difficult conversations strengthens not only your bond with your partner but also fosters stability for the children. When you stand together, you create an environment where children can thrive. They learn that boundaries are for their benefit, that love comes with responsibility, and that their parents are a team, united in their commitment to raising them well. This is how you transform a blended family into a cohesive unit.

Embrace the discomfort of those conversations. Understand that setting boundaries isn't just about discipline; it's about nurturing a culture of respect and accountability. Each time you and your partner align and communicate openly, you send a powerful message to your kids: We are in this together.

Celebrate the small victories along the way. Each time you reinforce a rule or navigate a challenge as a team, you're building a legacy of love, trust, and resilience. Your family will learn to rely on each other, and that bond—born from unity—will carry them through the ups and downs of life. You are not just a bonus mom; you are a cornerstone of a new family dynamic. Your strength, commitment, and willingness to show up for both your partner and his kids are what will ultimately transform this household into a loving home. Keep showing up, keep communicating, and remember that together, you are creating something not easy, but beautiful—a family that thrives on love and respect.

Letting Go of Control

Let me be brutally honest: letting go of control remains a challenge. It's a constant work in progress, both in my life and as a Badass Bonus Mom. For the first two years of this relationship—and I'm not exaggerating—I wrote Damon's text messages to his ex. I would sit there, crafting his words and managing their communication, believing that if I could control what he said, I could prevent conflict and smooth everything over, finally feeling like things were manageable. I was out of control trying to be in control.

The truth, which I didn't understand then, was that the more I tried to control the situation, the more out of control I felt. And the kids felt it, internalizing the conflict and feeling responsible for managing it. That realization hit hard. I realized you can't control the ex, dictate your partner's interactions with them, make the situation less awkward, or force them to respect your role. The only thing you can control is your response, and that's where your power lies.

You can't control custody schedule changes, the ex's parenting style, or what happens at their house. You can't control whether your bonus kids like, accept, or appreciate you. But you can control your reaction, the energy you bring to your home, and the peace you create when the kids are with you. When I stopped fighting to control things outside my power, I freed up energy to build something beautiful with what I actually had.

One day, Damon's ex said something that would have previously sent me spiraling. But this time, I just didn't care. I didn't text about it; I didn't replay it. I didn't let her control my mood. And you know what? The house felt different—calmer. The kids felt it. Damon felt it. Everything shifted because I finally stopped pulling so hard on a rope I could never control.

Letting go of control isn't just about relinquishing the reins; it's about reclaiming your peace and understanding that your strength lies not in manipulation but in acceptance. When you choose to let go, you open the door to a more authentic existence, allowing yourself to experience joy, laughter, and connection without unnecessary stress.

This shift creates a ripple effect. As you embrace your new reality, you model resilience and adaptability for the kids, showing them that life is unpredictable and that while we can't control every situation, we can choose how we respond. You become a living example of emotional strength, teaching them that their happiness doesn't hinge on external circumstances but on their inner peace.

So, as you navigate this complex journey, remember that true empowerment lies in your ability to adapt and respond thoughtfully. Be the guiding light in your home, illuminating the path with positivity and grace. Your ability to cultivate a peaceful environment, free from the chaos of things beyond your control, is what will ultimately strengthen your family bonds. Let go of the need to control and focus on nurturing the love and connection that truly matters. You are not just a Badass Bonus Mom; you are a force of nature. Embrace your power to create an atmosphere of love and stability, and watch as your family thrives in the warmth of your acceptance.

F-Bombs

There have been countless times I've felt like I was juggling flaming torches while putting out fires. Life is chaotic, messy, and sometimes downright frustrating. We're all human, and it's okay to feel overwhelmed. Those "f-bombs" (or whatever your go-to swear word is) are bound to happen. Bonus mom life doesn't come with a manual, and blending families means navigating a maze of emotions: yours, your partner's, and the kids'. It's a lot to handle.

While we can strive for grace and patience, there will be days when you need to let it out—and that's valid. When those f-bomb moments hit, recognize them as opportunities for growth. You might snap at your partner for forgetting something or lose your cool when the kids bicker. It happens! Instead of beating yourself up, take a step back and acknowledge the situation. You're allowed to feel frustrated, but the real power lies in how you respond. This isn't about avoiding those moments; it's about how you handle them afterward. Own your slip-ups, apologize if needed, and explain to the kids why you reacted that way. This teaches them that making mistakes is part of being human and that acknowledging them is a crucial life lesson.

I remember my first two f-bomb moments vividly: once when Bruno broke an irreplaceable, expensive martini glass—one of a set of four I'd bought, now reduced to three—that Damon had asked him to wash, and again when Rocco carelessly shattered a dish while washing it. I was frustrated because I had to teach them basic dish-washing skills they should have already known. It felt like they didn't see the effort I put into creating our home, and that stung. But the third time was different. I lost it over Bruno's disrespectful tone and Damon's "Disney Dad" approach, where he didn't hold his son accountable. I exploded: "Are you fucking kidding me? You do NOT get to talk to me that way, E-V-E-R! Do you understand me?" The look in their eyes made it clear—I was a force to be reckoned with. The silver lining? Those f-bomb moments sparked some of the best family discussions we've ever had. After each blow-up, we gathered to talk about what happened. I used it as a chance to teach the boys about emotions, how to express them, and how to communicate effectively. By transforming those challenging moments into learning opportunities, we fostered openness and understanding, strengthening our bond. Honestly, in the six years I've been a Badass Bonus Mom, I've dropped the f-bomb more times than I can count—something I'm not particularly proud of.

However, Bruno, Rocco, and I have had honest discussions about it, and they understand that when I use it, I mean business.

We've even shared a laugh about how one of my family catch-phrases, "I don't give a flying fuck," has become a running joke. As the boys have matured, and as I've given myself permission to take the breaks I need—girls' time with friends, visiting Kimberly in California, practicing yoga, etc.—those moments have become less frequent because I've learned to be more intentional with my reactions. When life gets heavy, laughter can be the best medicine. Embrace the chaos with a light heart. If you find yourself shouting in frustration, laugh it off and share the story later with your partner or friends. Those moments become funny anecdotes you'll cherish, turning into fond memories.

Managing those f-bomb moments requires one essential thing: self-care! You can't pour from an empty cup. When you're feeling overwhelmed, take a step back and recharge. Whether it's a few minutes of quiet time, a walk around the block, or indulging in your favorite TV show, find what restores your energy. By prioritizing self-care, you'll be better equipped to handle intense moments with grace and humor. As we navigate this journey together, remember that those f-bombs are simply part of the process. They don't define your worth as a bonus mom, partner, or person. Instead, they remind you that you're living life authentically, tackling challenges head-on with courage. At the end of the day, embrace those moments as part of your beautiful, chaotic life. I'm not condoning daily use—you're not a drunken sailor!

You're a bonus mom, capable of handling anything that comes your way, so give yourself grace. When the next curse word slips out, take a deep breath, scream, cry, laugh, and remind yourself that you're doing an amazing job. The fact that you care enough to feel bad about it is what truly makes you great. Making time for self-care also allows you to set realistic expectations.

Perfection isn't the goal, for you or your family. Life is messy, and that's okay. It's unrealistic to expect every day to be smooth sailing. Embrace the messiness, and don't hesitate to let the kids see you in your less-than-perfect moments. You're human, and they need to know that being real is perfectly fine. So here's to the curse words and all the messy moments that come with being a Badass Bonus Mom! Embrace them, learn from them, and remember that you are stronger than you think. Keep rocking this journey, and let your authenticity shine!

Flexibility

Happy Bonus Mom Day!
Love you for all you do to shape
the boys into fine young men!
Love you, Damon

Before we begin, let's be clear: being flexible doesn't mean you're a pushover. It means you're willing to compromise so that you, your partner, and your bonus kids all feel comfortable.

When Damon and I decided to move, I panicked. I'd lived in my condo for twenty-two years; it was my safe space, my anchor. Suddenly, I was supposed to leave it and navigate my bonus mom role in a house that felt enormous and unfamiliar, all while trying to co-parent effectively. I was terrified because I don't love change.

Damon didn't push me. Instead, he suggested we move in slowly: paint accent walls together, go furniture shopping together, and ease into it instead of forcing it. Over three months, we gradually brought pieces from the condo into the house. By the time the moving company arrived, I was ready and excited.

But here's what was beautiful: when Bruno and Rocco understood why moving had been so hard for me, something shifted. They saw me as human and realized that even adults get scared of change—just like they had when their parents divorced or adjusted to custody schedules. And they were there, cheering me on. That's the power of letting your bonus kids in on your process.

Flexibility is essential in blended families. Plans change, schedules shift, and last-minute custody adjustments happen. When you can roll with it instead of resist it, you model resilience for everyone. If a planned family outing gets rained out and turns into a cozy night in, lean into it. Saying, "Let's make the best of this," can turn disappointment into a cherished memory.

Change strips away the superficial and gets to the heart of who you're going to be as a family. When you navigate change together, you're not just surviving it; you're building trust, deepening bonds, and creating a family identity that's uniquely yours as their bonus mom. That's true strength.

Embracing flexibility empowers you to shape your family's narrative. It's a potent reminder that life inevitably throws curveballs, but your response defines the essence of your relationships. Each adaptation teaches your bonus kids invaluable lessons: uncertainty is acceptable, transformation can be beautiful, and love remains constant.

By cultivating flexibility, you're not simply accommodating change; you're fostering growth and resilience within your family. Show your bonus kids that change is an adventure, not a setback. Teach them that every twist can lead to new opportunities for connection and joy. Lean into the unexpected and celebrate life's spontaneity. Each shared moment—whether in a new house or navigating life's surprises—builds a stronger, more unified family. Your adaptability is a gift, empowering those around you and reinforcing that together, you can face anything. You are a Bad-Ass Bonus Mom, and your ability to embrace change with grace and positivity will ultimately create a loving and resilient family. Keep shining; your flexibility is a strength that will guide you through every season.

Crafting a Unique Family Legacy

Before entering a relationship, we often have cherished traditions—celebrating holidays with friends or family, relishing the warmth of gatherings during Easter, Thanksgiving, Hanukkah, Christmas, New Year's, or Chinese New Year. Becoming a bonus mom changes everything.

As a bonus mom, your traditions may evolve, adapt, or transform, shaped by your family's unique blend of identities. This presents a beautiful opportunity to honor the past while creating something entirely new.

I was eager to carry forward the ritual of making homemade apple pie, a tradition I cherished with my late grandmother just before Thanksgiving. It was a meaningful connection to my roots. I also wanted to incorporate the joyful memory of Christmas mornings spent with my late dad (my dad passed away when I was 20 years old), making blueberry pancakes while listening to Gladys Knight and the Pips' "Midnight Train to Georgia." I can still visualize my dad's smile as he danced with my siblings and me, while my mom swayed to the rhythm. These memories aren't just nostalgia; they're the threads weaving through our family's fabric.

When Damon and I celebrated our first Christmas together, we broke from tradition and chose lasagna instead of the typical holiday feast. This decision followed a Thanksgiving that overlapped with our anniversary, which we spent away. Initially, the boys were hesitant; they were accustomed to their mother's mouthwatering beef tenderloin. But Damon and I wanted to establish a new tradition for our little family. So, lasagna became our Christmas centerpiece.

Now, every year, we prepare lasagna the weekend before Christmas. We decorate the dining room, creating a festive atmosphere that enhances the spirit of the season and celebrate a "family Christmas" with Damon's dad, his wife Mary, and his sister Brittany with her husband and son, filling our home with laughter and holiday cheer.

As a family, Damon, Bruno, Rocco, and I gather to put up our Christmas tree, hanging ornaments while sipping eggnog and playing holiday music—another cherished tradition from my upbringing. We hang stockings with our names, a nod to Damon's family customs. On Christmas morning, we indulge in blueberry pancakes, accompanied by my favorite song that Damon and I slow dance to, and wear holiday onesies or matching pajamas.

The boys continue their tradition of watching holiday movies, including classics like *The Sound of Music* and *A Christmas Story*, either with their mom or us, depending on the year. Over the years, we've also made it a point to watch *The Family Stone*—my favorite holiday movie, which has cemented its place in our repertoire. To keep things lighthearted, Damon and I even added a holiday-themed horror movie to our Christmas morning ritual—just to keep everyone laughing!

We also make holiday cookies together, allowing the boys to decorate them before sharing them with our neighbors, fostering a sense of community.

On Easter, after church, we celebrate with a hearty brunch, and each child receives an Easter basket filled with treats.

The beauty of traditions lies in their power to connect us—to our past, to each other, and to the future we're building. There are countless ways to create traditions that reflect your personality and your partner's, allowing you to weave a unique tapestry of experiences for your family. These traditions are vital; they instill a sense of belonging and value, creating a home that celebrates individuality and the love you share as a blended family.

Embrace the opportunity to craft new traditions and breathe life into old ones. As a Badass Bonus Mom, you have the chance to create a legacy that honors the past while paving the way for the future. Your unique family story is waiting to be written— make it beautiful.

Celebrate It All

Welcome Home Princess!
The Home Is Not The Same Without You.
**and behind on bad television :)*
Love, Damon

When I started planning Bruno's graduation party, I was excited but also terrified of messing it up. Without kids of my own, my experience with children's parties was limited to birthday celebrations for Bruno and Rocco. I excelled at planning birthday parties and celebrations for Damon and my close friends, as well as other adult gatherings—holiday parties, dinner parties, and surprise parties—but a graduation party felt like new territory. What if Bruno didn't like it, or his friends didn't have fun? What if I forgot something important? As the party date approached, I kept second-guessing myself. Should I plan something extravagant, or keep it low-key? Would he think I was trying too hard? Damon finally told me to just do what felt right, and I realized that what felt right was the same thing I do for everyone I love: make it meaningful.

So, I ordered cupcakes from his favorite bakery. I created a poster board with photos of Bruno, from when I first met him until his graduation year. I bought candy, desserts, and decorations in his future college's colors. I made food, got drinks, balloons, and paper goods, and chose gifts that mattered—things that showed I actually knew him, not just whatever was on sale.

When the day arrived, we celebrated him the way we celebrate everyone we love in this family: we showed up, fully present. That's when I understood that celebration is how you build family. Before, I thought celebrating meant big parties and expensive gifts; I thought it had to be grand to matter. But then I started paying attention to what actually worked.

One Saturday, after Rocco's lacrosse game—not a championship, just a regular game where he'd played hard—Damon said, "Let's get burgers." No special occasion, no trophy, just a way of saying, "We saw you. We're proud of you. Let's acknowledge it." We did that after several of Bruno's and Rocco's games, win or lose. And both boys started looking for us in the stands differently, not because we were the loudest or most enthusiastic, but because we were consistent. Because we showed up and celebrated the effort, not just the outcome.

That ritual—the post-game burgers, the high-fives, the specific words we'd use about what we'd just saw them do—transformed us from a dad, his girlfriend, and kids into a real family. I'm a planner; I love the details. And I realized long ago that I show love by paying attention to what matters to people and then honoring it with intention. It's not about expensive gifts, but about gifts that say, "I know you. I see you. This is why." When Bruno graduated high school, I spent over two months planning his graduation party—not the typical, expected "graduation party," but a celebration that reflected who he is and how proud

I am of who he's becoming. I thought about what would make him feel seen, what details would matter to him, and how to make the day feel like it was built just for him, because it was. And he knew it. That's the power of intentional celebration. It doesn't have to be expensive or elaborate, but it has to mean something.

I've learned that the celebrations that stick are also the small ones: the moment you notice your kid cleaned their room without being asked, and you stop what you're doing to say, "I see you. I'm proud of that." It's the random Wednesday when everyone actually got along, and you call a "family dance party" just to mark the occasion. These moments say something powerful: In this family, we notice the good stuff. We don't just survive the chaos—we celebrate the connection. I think a lot of blended families miss this: celebrating together is literally how you turn separate people into a real family. When you celebrate your bonus kid's win like it's your own, something shifts. When you show up for your partner's accomplishments, when you acknowledge the hard days your bonus kid had and celebrate that they survived it, you're sending a message that says, "You belong here. Your life matters. We're in this together." That's not performative; that's foundational.

As you navigate this journey, remember that every celebration—big or small—adds to the foundation of your family. Each time you acknowledge a moment, you're weaving connections that will last a lifetime. Think of yourself as the architect of joy, crafting spaces where love thrives and laughter echoes.

Ladies, when I first became a published author, my partner threw me a party, gave a speech, and presented me with a meaningful card.

*Princess, I love that we are celebrating you being
published in a book for women. I know this has been a
dream, and now it is a dream come true.
I am very proud of you. Keep it going and
you will be a huge success. You are AMAZING!
Love Damon*

Cultivate a culture of celebration within your home, one that resonates through every room. Forget perfection; embrace presence. Show up with an open heart, choosing to recognize the beauty in everyday moments. So, celebrate—whether it's a graduation, a small victory, or simply a Tuesday! Make it special, and let your bonus kids know their lives are worth celebrating. Be the spark that ignites joy, the cheerleader who lifts them up, and the heart that binds your family together. By choosing to celebrate, you're not just marking occasions; you're building a legacy of love and connection that will resonate for years to come. And that, dear Badass Bonus Moms, is the real gift you're giving—not just to them, but to yourself. Embrace this journey and know that you are not just part of a blended family; you are its heartbeat. Celebrate it all, unapologetically!

The Family You Didn't Plan But Absolutely Need

*Merry Christmas Michelle! Thanks for the great year.
I'm extremely grateful for all you do! Love, Bruno.*

I was in the kitchen making coffee when Bruno walked in and
asked for my opinion on a marketing project for school—he asked
me, not his dad. He sat at the island, sharing his ideas while I
listened. In that moment, I realized, *This is the payoff*. Not in an
"I've finally earned my stripes" way, but in a "this kid trusts me
enough to value my opinion" way. Two years earlier, I wouldn't
have believed it possible. Let's be honest about that first year. I
was doing laundry for two teenage boys—plus Damon, when
Rocco visited. I was cleaning and cooking, with Damon's help.
I was negotiating bedtimes. I was doing most of the grocery
shopping. I was the boundaries, accountabilities, and consequences enforcer. I was navigating a co-parenting minefield
with a woman who wouldn't acknowledge my existence. I was
watching my partner struggle to be present—before the kids

moved in—because he didn't know how to juggle being a dad and a partner to me. I was exhausted—genuinely, bone-deep exhausted. And I wasn't getting paid or benefits or coffee breaks. I was getting eye-rolls and a few "You're not my mom" moments that landed like punches. Some days, I looked at Damon and wondered, *What the hell did I sign up for?* I'd given up my routine, my privacy, the ability to simply exist in my own home without thinking about someone else's schedule, needs, or emotions. The price was real, and it was steep. A shift occurred that I didn't see coming.

One day, Bruno came home from school and, instead of seeking out his dad, he came to me. He was upset about something that had happened, and rather than retreating to his room or calling his mom, he sat down next to me and started talking. Although it wasn't the first time he'd sought my opinion or advice, this time felt different, more personal. I remember looking at him—this kid who'd been a stranger when he first started living with his dad and me in my condo—and realizing, *He trusts ME.* Not because I'd earned it through obligation, or because I was an authority figure, but because I'd shown up consistently. I'd been present. I'd listened without judgment. I'd cared about his life in a way that had nothing to do with being his bonus mom and everything to do with simply caring. That was the first moment I felt the payoff, or the day Rocco hugged me first, before leaving to go back to his mom's—without me asking or initiating it. These small moments started adding up, and I realized this is what I was actually signing up for, and I had no idea the magnitude of love I could have for both Bruno and Rocco.

Here's what nobody tells you: when you commit to being a Badass Bonus Mom, you're not just gaining a partner and kids;

you're creating something that doesn't fit into traditional family boxes. You're not their mom, but you're not "just" a parent figure either. You're the woman who knows their school schedule better than they do. You're the one who remembers their food preferences and allergies. You're the one who listens to their problems without trying to fix everything—Switzerland parenting! You're the one who shows up to their games, recitals, and graduations. You're the one who sees them—*really* sees them—and loves them anyway. You're the one who has conversations with them about growing up, relationships, and disappointment. You're the one they come to when they need advice that might be too vulnerable to ask their parents for. You're creating a family dynamic that's uniquely yours—not better than other families, just different, just real. In our case, it meant that Bruno and Rocco had three adults who loved them: their mom, their dad, and me. It meant they had different kinds of support, different perspectives, different strengths. It meant they weren't just getting parenting; they were getting mentorship from multiple people who cared. It meant that when Bruno needed advice, he could come to me because I understood in a way his dad couldn't. It meant that when Rocco needed to feel like part of our family—even though he lived with his mom full-time—I made a point of showing him, without him having to ask. I'd have his favorite foods ready when he arrived and special gifts during holidays. It meant our family wasn't traditional, but it was exactly what we all needed.

Merry new year! Rocco

I want to be clear: the payoff wasn't one big moment, not a dramatic scene where everyone suddenly realizes they're a family. It was the accumulation of small moments that added up to something real, like the night we were all watching a movie together—me, Damon, Bruno, and Rocco—and nobody was on their phone, nobody pretending to be somewhere else. We were just together, laughing at the same jokes, comfortable in the silence between us, or when Bruno introduced me to his friend at school as "my stepmom" with a tone that conveyed pride, not awkward explanation, as if he was claiming me, or when Rocco asked me to send him a photo of himself, his dad, Bruno, and me—all together for a family school project, or when Bruno, who'd struggled with the divorce and the blended family, told me that having me around made his dad happier, which in turn made him happier—that my presence had actually improved his life instead of complicating it. It was our yearly Christmas dinner with Bruno, Rocco, and Damon's family and the traditions we'd created, which had become our family rituals, not my obligation. It was when I stopped feeling like I was performing the role of bonus mom and started just being part of the family, when it stopped being something I was doing and started being something I was.

All that exhaustion, all that sacrifice, all those moments when I wanted to quit—they weren't wasted. They were building something: trust that I would show up, even when it was hard; trust that I wouldn't bail when things got complicated; trust that I actually cared about their lives, not just the logistics of them. We were building a relationship that had nothing to do with obligation and everything to do with choice. These kids didn't have to let me in. Nobody forced them to. But they did, slowly, over time, because I kept showing up. We were building a family dynamic that's genuinely unique, not perfect, but real, messy, complicated, and beautiful in ways only blended families can be. In the process, I discovered I was capable of so much more than

I thought. I learned patience I didn't know I possessed. I learned to advocate for kids who weren't biologically mine and to love fiercely and vulnerably. I learned to navigate complexity with grace—most days. It took time, but Damon started to understand and appreciate what I was actually doing. For a long time, he thought I was being too strict at times with his kids, not realizing I was building a relationship. He didn't see the emotional labor or understand that I was choosing to be present in a way that required constant vulnerability. But then he watched my relationship with Rocco develop. He watched me help Bruno navigate anxiety and friendship drama. He watched me make their favorite meals, plan their celebrations, and show up for them in small ways that added up to something big. Eventually, he thanked me for all the hard work I'd put in. That mattered, not because I needed his approval, but because my partner finally understood that I wasn't just his girlfriend anymore; I was a parent. And that shifted how he showed up, too.

Stephanie. Thank you for your caring heart. All the love & understanding you have given me from day one. You mean more to me than I can even express. You have my heart & soul. This has been so fun pulling this Christmas together. You have made our House A Home.
Love Damon

Damon started being more present, backing me up, and being a partner in this, not just a bystander watching his girlfriend take care of his kids. That was part of the payoff, too. When I first met Damon, I wasn't looking for kids or to upend my entire life. I was just looking for a partner. What I got was a partner and a family that changed me. I got a teenager who trusts me enough to confide in me and a kid who lights up when he sees me. I got a household that's chaotic, exhausting, and sometimes frustrating—and also full of inside jokes, random dance parties, and moments of genuine connection. I got a life that's nothing like what I planned, and somehow it's exactly what I needed. The payoff isn't that everything became easy, but that the hard stuff became worth it. The sacrifices started to feel like active choices, not something I was suffering through because this is my family, these are my people, and I'm exactly where I'm supposed to be. Ladies, the family you're building as a Badass Bonus Mom isn't going to look like anyone else's. It's not going to fit neatly into boxes or follow traditional rules, and that's the whole point. You're creating something that's only possible because you chose to show up, to love fiercely, and to be present even when it was hard.

You're showing these kids what commitment and follow-through look like. You're showing them that family isn't just about biology—it's about presence, effort, and choosing each other. When you do that consistently, over time, something shifts, and the payoff comes. It doesn't come all at once, but it arrives in small moments that accumulate into something significant, in trust earned through presence, in a uniquely beautiful family dynamic that's a gift worth cherishing.

Embrace every moment, both challenging and beautiful. Allow the process to unfold organically, knowing that each step is a testament to your strength and commitment. Celebrate the unpredictability of your new family, for it is in that unpredictability that the most profound connections are forged. Remember, you're not just a bonus mom; you're a vital thread woven into the fabric of this family. Your love, patience, and dedication are creating a legacy of compassion and resilience. Each time you choose to show up, you reinforce that love transcends traditional definitions of family. So, keep nurturing those connections, embracing the chaos, and showing up with an open heart. You are part of something truly special—something that, despite its challenges, will enrich your life in unexpected ways. The family you didn't plan but absolutely needed is here, and it's a beautiful journey worth every moment.

A Journey That Keeps Building

For many, co-parenting someone else's children without marriage or engagement can be a tough sell for many, primarily because nothing is guaranteed. You might wait for marriage only to discover you don't connect with your partner's kids. Or, even if married, you might think, "His kids, his responsibility." Realistically, there's nothing wrong with either approach—do what works for you.

As we've learned, being a bonus mom isn't for the faint of heart. You're choosing to take on a significant role in your already busy life without the assurance that you and your partner will be "together forever." However, here's my theory: if marriage is your aspiration, becoming a bonus mom can help you and your partner determine if marriage is right for you, without the constraints of paperwork or the potential for an early divorce.

It's amusing to observe people's reactions when I call Bruno and Rocco my stepsons or bonus kids. They're often confused when I explain that Damon and I aren't married. "Why?" is usually the first question, followed by, "So how are they your step-kids?" It's as if a ring is the only validation that counts, yet people readily claim their pets as family members!

I vividly recall Bruno's first orthodontist appointment. After we checked in, the dental assistant called him back to take photos. As I settled into the waiting area, she turned to me, smiling warmly, and asked, "Hi, Bruno's mom, would you like to join him?" My heart swelled with pride, and I immediately stood up, but before I could explain that I was his dad's girlfriend, Bruno, his face lighting up, gently said, "It's okay."

The moment made me chuckle, as it happens often. It's amusing how people perceive our connection, though a closer look makes it easy to see why. Bruno has thick, dark, wavy curls, a blend of his dad's and mine. He's lean and has a wider nose like mine, but otherwise, his face resembles Damon's. Even though we aren't blood-related, we are energetically connected.

As an adoptee, I'm always touched when people comment on how much I look like my adoptive mother, who raised me. It's equally heartwarming when others recognize the bond between Bruno and me, seeing us as "son and bonus mom." It's a testament to the love and connection we share, one that transcends traditional labels and speaks to the beauty of our blended family.

During one of our many sushi outings with Damon and the boys when Bruno asked if he could tweak a roll I was ordering. The server looked at me and asked, "Is that okay with your mom?" Damon didn't even flinch. I just smiled and said, "Yes, that's fine." After the server walked away, Bruno chuckled, saying it was funny how many people assumed I was his mom.

When I asked if I should correct them, he quickly replied, "No, I'm okay with it."

Bruno and I share a bond that transcends labels. He calls me "Michelle" wherever we go, but our connection shines through, leading others to assume our relationship. To be clear, Bruno's acceptance of this perception isn't a slight against his mom, whom he loves dearly. Correcting everyone who assumes I'm his mom would be exhausting. Ultimately, the essence of our relationship matters more than titles.

I deeply cherish the honor of being welcomed into Bruno's life and trusted by him. Together, we've grown and become better because of our unique family bond. I owe Damon a great deal of gratitude for facilitating this connection. As a bonus mom, you understand why you embarked on this incredible journey, filled with emotional highs and lows. You know what you're building and the self-sacrifices you're making. Keep building your family! Create a strong and secure foundation. If marriage is your ultimate desire, be honest with your partner, but don't let that stop you from being the Badass Bonus Mom you were meant to be.

In a world where divorces are commonplace, the bond you create with your bonus kids is a forever journey. Remember, your role as a bonus mom is invaluable. You are shaping lives and making an impact that goes beyond traditional definitions of family. Embrace this beautiful path, knowing that the love and connection you forge today will be the foundation for tomorrow's adventures. You are not just a step in their journey; you are a vital part of their story.

The Unspoken Promise

Ladies, let's be honest: being a Badass Bonus Mom is hard work. You might have thought you signed up for a fun adventure—and, at first, you kind of did. But what you're really getting is a full-time job with overtime—without paychecks, benefits, or even a coffee break sometimes. Welcome to the party. Here's something nobody tells you: finding a partner who's actively involved in his kids' lives is like finding a unicorn. It's possible, but rare. And if your guy is more of a Disney Dad—swooping in with charm and the latest gaming console while you're stuck with homework, chores, and the eternal "Why can't I have potato chips for breakfast?" debates—well, congratulations, you've officially won the exhaustion lottery.

The heavy lifting falls on you. You become the primary caregiver, navigating the tantrums, the eye-rolls, and the teenage angst. Weekends transform from lingerie and good books to lacrosse games, carpooling, and stealing five minutes of "me time" whenever you can. Your life changes in ways you absolutely did not sign up for.

But here's where it gets interesting: it gets better. With the right partner and kids who are meant to be in your life, those changes are actually worth it. I know that's not what you want to hear when you're drowning in homework or disciplinary drama, but stick with me.

I remember when Bruno was finally ready to cut the hair he had been hiding behind. He asked if my stylist could cut his hair and if I could supervise the haircut, based on the photos we looked at online. Not only did he trust me—which made me want to scream with excitement—but his haircut also symbolized the deeper bond, trust, and connection we had built. Bruno is such a handsome young man, and to see him come out of his shell, wanting me to be a part of it, felt like he was saying, "I trust you, and I know you are here for me." Finally, it felt like Bruno was truly accepting me.

Being a bonus mom means one minute you're bonding over ice cream and movies, and the next, you're navigating complex co-parenting dynamics with a biological mother you never asked to have in your life. It's like performing a delicate ballet while juggling flaming torches—exciting, yet terrifying. Somehow, you manage to keep from dropping anything, most days. Then, something shifts. Your bonus kid starts coming home and telling you about their day first—before they tell their dad. They ask for your advice instead of running to their biological parent. They write you a meaningful message in a card and call you by a special name, a name that's just theirs for you. That's when you realize: this is exactly where you're supposed to be!

Your life becomes this beautiful, chaotic mixture of things you never expected to care about. You transform into a multitasking wizard, balancing work, your social life, and the demands of being a bonus mom all at once. You master the art of packing school lunches while simultaneously negotiating bedtimes like a seasoned diplomat. You attend more sports games than you thought humanly possible and discover that you actually care who wins. You develop a deeper understanding of how kids think, how they feel, and the quirky ways they show love. You also discover that you're capable of so much more than you ever imagined.

You learn to appreciate the little victories: a heartfelt hug, a moment of laughter over a silly movie, a "thank you" that catches you off guard because you weren't expecting it. These small moments start to add up, becoming the fabric of your relationship with these kids. The messy, chaotic, and exhausting reality of it all means that some days you'll wonder what you were thinking. Some days you'll feel undervalued and overwhelmed. Some days you'll want to quit. But then your bonus kid will run to show you their art project, or they'll ask your opinion on something important, or they'll defend you to their friend or even to their parents. And you'll remember why you're doing this.

Your life as a bonus mom might not look like what you envisioned when you first decided to blend families. It won't be perfect. There will be moments of doubt, days when you question everything, and times when you feel like you're failing. That's real life, and it's completely normal. But here's the beautiful part: you're creating something incredibly special. You're building a blended family where love knows no bounds, showing your bonus kids what it looks like to be committed, to show up, and to care even when things are challenging. You're teaching them that family isn't about biology but about presence, effort, and choosing each other.

Damon, the boys, and I embarked on family bike rides—a venture I initially resisted, having not been on a bike in over twenty years. Contrary to the saying, "It's just like riding a bike," I assure you, that wasn't the case for me. Damon and Rocco would speed off as if in a competitive race, while Bruno stayed by my side, protecting me as he rode behind. He noticed my nervousness and discomfort, a stark contrast to my childhood when I rode bikes for years, conquering steep hills and navigating our neighborhood with ease. Bruno guided me with clear instructions and a gentle, caring tone. He rang his bell to alert others when I was too anxious, spoke soothingly to ease my stress, and when I almost crashed into another rider, he calmly reassured me that it happens. He advised me to avoid looking at oncoming bikes, explaining that my bike would instinctively veer in that direction, and he encouraged me every step of the way.

Tears fill my eyes as I write this because, Badass Bonus Moms, that is unconditional love. It's genuine care that fills our household and lives with warmth, even through challenging moments. The hard work you're putting in right now? It matters. The love you're giving? It matters. The sacrifices you're making? They matter. Because when you have the right partner and kids who are meant to be in your life, those changes you're making—the chaos, the exhaustion, the messy, beautiful journey—are absolutely worth it.

You're not just a bonus mom. You're a Badass Bonus Mom, and your life is becoming an incredible adventure woven with love, laughter, and the occasional chaos. And here's the truth: every moment you invest in these relationships is a seed planted for the future. As you nurture them, you're cultivating resilience, empathy, and connection that will resonate for years to come. You are creating a legacy that transcends traditional family norms, one where love and choice define your bond.

So, embrace the challenges and celebrate the victories, both big and small. Know that your journey is uniquely yours, filled with experiences that will shape not only your bonus kids but also the incredible person you are becoming. You are crafting a family that is diverse, vibrant, and full of love.

And remember, even on the toughest days, you are not alone. You are part of a community of Badass Bonus Moms navigating this same path, and together, you are changing lives. Hold your head high and wear that title with pride. You are not just a bonus mom; you are an essential part of something truly extraordinary.

Love Wins

Bonus Mom, have you ever wondered how your bonus kids truly feel about you? Instead of guessing based on heartfelt cards or thoughtful gifts, why not ask them directly? I cherish the moments I tell my bonus sons, Bruno and Rocco, that I love them. While writing down what I appreciate about them is meaningful, expressing it face-to-face is even more powerful. During our trip to Costa Rica in 2021, the boys wrote down ten things they loved about their dad and me. Five years later, as they've grown and we've spent more time building our family foundation, I decided to ask them for an updated list of what they love most about me.

Bruno's List:
- ★ You give great advice.
- ★ Very easy to talk to.
- ★ Fun to hang out with.

★ You are a safe place to go to.
★ Never boring.
★ Good cook.
★ Very understanding.
★ Holds me to a higher standard.
★ Always there for me.
★ Funny.

Rocco's List:
★ You are always there when I need someone to talk to.
★ You have a great sense of humor.
★ You listen to me and actually care about what I say.
★ You support me and encourage me to do my best.
★ You are honest and trustworthy.
★ You treat others with respect.
★ You stay positive even during tough times.
★ You make time to spend with me.
★ You help me when I'm struggling.
★ You inspire me to be a better person.

Ladies, reading these lists brought tears to my eyes. Through laughter, tears, celebrations, roller coaster rides, and heartfelt moments, I've made a significant impact on their lives, just as they have on mine. The gratitude is profound. Whether you're contemplating becoming a bonus mom, are already on this journey, or are questioning the impact you're making, know that you are on the right path. Connections can be forged, bonds can deepen, and before you know it, you'll become a Badass Bonus Mom who deserves recognition for opening your heart and embracing all the challenges and joys that come with it. You are making a difference—one moment, one laugh, and one act of love at a time. Remember, each day is a new opportunity to inspire and uplift, not just your bonus kids but yourself as well. Embrace the beautiful chaos, celebrate the small victories, and know that your love and dedication are shaping their lives in ways you may not even realize, like the fact that Bruno said I'm a good cook. You have the power to create a legacy of love, resilience, and connection that will last a lifetime. So keep shining your light, for in the tapestry of family, your threads are woven with strength and beauty.

Your New Sparkle

Good luck with your back surgery tmrw,
Love Rocco

Before stepping into the role of a Badass Bonus Mom, you radiated an undeniable glow. Your face was radiant, your hair thick and vibrant, and your smile magnetic. You felt sexy and strong, enjoying the freedom to work out whenever you wanted—whether it was yoga, Pilates, or a good jog. You slept soundly, and the twinkle in your rested eyes reflected your energy. You felt like you were living your best life.

But let's be honest: kids can drain, frankly, suck your energy and youth. I said it! Many women think this but hesitate to voice it, fearing they'll be labeled a bad mom. You're not bad; having these feelings is completely normal and doesn't diminish your love for your kids. As a Badass Bonus Mom, you might not be changing diapers, but you are juggling a different set of complexities, which brings its own stress, pressure, and challenges. You're dealing with the emotional aftermath of divorce, the growing pains of transitioning teenagers, and all the hormonal shifts that come with it. Add in homework help, sports activities, carpooling, and being the designated chauffeur (especially if you live somewhere without school buses). Navigating boundaries, accountability, and discipline while figuring out your role in their lives—just writing about it is exhausting!

I remember my sister, Tanya, Kimberly, and I joking, "Why do I feel like I'm aging at warp speed?" and "Where has all the time gone?" We'd laugh because if we didn't, we might just cry. But deep down, we weren't entirely joking. Looking in the mirror, I noticed tired eyes—now needing to wear my glasses daily (versus pre-kids)—now dull skin, and thinning hair with too many gray strands trying to appear too soon. I have major TMJ (temporomandibular joint) disorder, causing my teeth to shift due to nighttime jaw-clenching stress. Me!—who had almost perfect teeth needed Invisalign in my 50s. My clothes didn't fit the same because I hadn't worked out in months, and I found myself pouring a glass of wine more often just to get through the day. Don't get me wrong, I'm not saying that kids cause blindness—that's ridiculous! However, the evidence was clear.

At first, I thought I was being overly critical of myself, but when I compared photos from before my relationship, during it, and from when I first became a bonus mom to now—almost eight years in—I realized my sparkle had visibly changed. As much as I love Bruno and Rocco and am grateful they are unknowingly in my life, the children dimmed my glow, partly because I allowed it. Being a Badass Bonus Mom takes extra effort—sometimes more than parenting your own children, if you have them. You're navigating the lives of kids who are independent and have opinions shaped by their other parent, which can sometimes feel annoying or frustrating. You're getting to know them while also deepening your relationship with your partner. You're managing expectations, setting boundaries, and figuring out your place in their lives. That's a lot to process, and it shows. But here's what I've learned: your sparkle doesn't disappear; it transforms. The glow you had before was real, but the strength, resilience, and depth you're building now create a different kind of sparkle—one earned through love, sacrifice, and showing up even on the toughest days.

Self-care isn't just a luxury; it's essential for a Badass Bonus Mom. I wish someone had drilled this into my head early on—a mentor who could say, "You need to protect your energy, or you will lose yourself." I get it now. To reclaim some of my glow, I make it a point to visit my best friend Kimberly in Laguna Beach two to four times a year. Our beach walks and ocean chats are my rejuvenating oasis. Getaways with Damon twice a year help too—whether it's a weekend road trip to Santa Fe or a beach escape to Mexico, Florida, or California. These aren't just indulgences; they're survival tools. But here's the key: you don't need to wait for a girls' trip or a vacation to reclaim your sparkle. It starts with small choices. It begins with acknowledging that you matter just as much as the kids and your partner. It involves saying no to things that drain you and yes to what fills your cup. Remember, taking care of yourself isn't selfish—it's necessary. Your sparkle is still there. It hasn't vanished; it's just been buried under exhaustion and the beautiful chaos of blended family life, waiting for you to reclaim it. When you prioritize yourself and your well-being, your glow will return, and you'll model for the kids that self-love and respect are essential. You'll show them what a Badass Bonus Mom really looks like: someone who gives fiercely while also protecting her own peace.

So go take that walk. Schedule that coffee with your "Kimberly." Book that weekend trip. Work out when you feel like it. Let your hair down—literally and figuratively. Your sparkle is still yours; it's just evolved into something deeper, stronger, and more radiant.

Treasure Each Moment

Sorry I didn't say goodbye I didn't want to interrupt your podcast. I love you and thanks for letting me go up to the mtns this weekend. Bruno

In 2019, Bruno and Rocco entered my life, and I had no idea I was about to embark on the wild ride of being a bonus mom—a Badass Bonus Mom, to be precise. Time has flown by. It feels like just yesterday that I welcomed them, yet the memories we've created are treasures I hold dear. That's why it's essential to savor every moment, take plenty of photos, and appreciate this incredible journey.

In 2019, when I first met Bruno, he was finishing eighth grade and deciding which high school to attend. I remember in October 2020, we went to the Dumb Friends League to adopt a kitten, and he walked around wide-eyed, trying to decide which one he wanted. After looking at several kittens that didn't feel quite right, I finally picked one, and Bruno was so excited to hold our newest fur-baby, Luna—a name he chose. Now he's already finishing his college sophomore year! Rocco, who was finishing fourth grade then, is now a high school sophomore, soon to be a junior. Watching these two boys grow into remarkable young men is astonishing, like watching a captivating series unfold, complete with plot twists and character development!

These days, since Bruno is away at school in Montana, my conversations with him usually take place over the phone or FaceTime. Hearing the excitement bubble in Bruno's voice as he spoke about coming home for spring break filled me with so much joy, and I began counting down the days until I saw him. Meanwhile, Rocco is still playing lacrosse, demonstrating how far he's come since his days as a tiny, fierce player. My heart swells with pride, knowing that all the hard work, sacrifices, laughter, and love we shared have truly paid off.

Remember those days when chores felt like a battle? Last year, Bruno called to tell me how he keeps his fraternity room clean and appreciates why I was so strict about maintaining his space. It's moments like those that remind you that your efforts are recognized and valued—even if they weren't always appreciated at the time.

The teenage years can feel like a dramatic rollercoaster, filled with hormones and emotional highs and lows. But somehow, they zip through middle school and high school, and before you know it, you're celebrating graduations. You throw parties, take photos of Homecoming dances and proms, cheer for their achievements, and then suddenly find yourself packing up their things for college, tears welling up as reality sinks in.

When Bruno first set off for college, I was a blubbering mess. I had been so giddy about the freedom his absence would bring—finally, more alone time and date nights with Damon! But as moving day approached, it hit me hard: my baby, who had lived with us full-time, was leaving the nest. I could still picture that first day when he looked up at me with his big brown eyes, asking if he could stay with us. Flashbacks flooded my mind: Bruno's first haircut, his ridiculous dance moves to *that* song, family walks, disciplinary moments, countless hugs, and those f-bombs that occasionally slipped out during family fun. From basketball games at the park to teaching the boys about hygiene, workout sessions at the gym, bowling nights, and holiday celebrations, every moment was a thread in the tapestry of our lives together. Looking back, that day feels like both a million years ago and just yesterday. We often hear phrases like "savor every moment" or "time flies," but you don't truly grasp their meaning until you become a parent or a bonus parent.

The speed at which children grow and change is staggering, and the impact you have on their lives—good or bad—is monumental. When we first became empty-nesters, our home felt eerily quiet. Damon and I struggled to find our groove without Bruno's vibrant energy. It felt strange, even though we knew he was just off at college. The dynamics of our family had shifted, leaving me uncertain about how to redirect my time and energy after investing so much love into kids who had transformed from strangers into cherished family members. But here's the empowering truth: this shift is a positive sign. It means you've done your job well, and your kids are ready to spread their wings. Just because they're off on their own doesn't mean they don't need you anymore; the phone calls won't stop, and the connection won't fade. This is simply the beginning of a new chapter where spontaneous vacations and quality time with your partner can take center stage once again.

Damon and I now eagerly await our Sunday FaceTime calls with Bruno, and each visit from Rocco, although less frequent due to high school sports, lights up our day. These moments are precious gifts that we cherish deeply. This bonus mom journey has transformed my life in ways I can hardly articulate. My heart has expanded in ways I never imagined possible, and I have no regrets about any part of this miraculous adventure.

Every challenge and triumph has shaped us, weaving a beautiful tapestry of family and love. As you continue your own bonus mom journey, treasure each moment. Celebrate the milestones, embrace the changes, and remember that you are doing an incredible job. Your love and dedication lay the groundwork for the amazing futures that lie ahead for your bonus kids. As they embark on new adventures, know that your role as a Badass Bonus Mom is *more vital than ever.* Keep shining, keep loving, and let every moment inspire you as you navigate this extraordinary path together! Grab your camera, your tissues, and your sense of humor, because this journey is just getting started, and there are many more beautiful moments to create!

The Magic of Being a Bonus Mom

"Thank you for all you have done for my dad and me. You have made this whole situation and the divorce so much better. Thank you. Can't wait to see you Monday." This simple message from Bruno perfectly captures the magic of being a bonus mom. When I began dating my partner, I never imagined that navigating the complexities of loving his children would lead to such profound self-discovery. Yet, here I am, feeling incredibly fortunate and realizing that true love flourishes in the quiet, un-Instagrammed moments cherished in the heart.

Let's be honest: becoming a bonus mom wasn't on my life's to-do list. I certainly wasn't thinking, "Parenting someone else's kids without legal authority or consistent recognition, and dealing with an ex-wife who undermines rather than appreciates another adult loving her kids, is exactly what my life needs!" But then, life took a beautiful turn. I fell deeply in love with a man who had two incredible kids. Somewhere in the whirlwind of school runs and sports games, I realized something that still amazes me: I am the luckiest woman in the world.

Sorry if I disrespected you yesterday. I really didn't mean to come off that way. I want to talk to you after school, and I am really sorry about how I've been all summer. —Bruno

It hasn't been easy; God knows it hasn't. I've cried in my car or bedroom closet more times than I can count, feeling replaced, undervalued, and overwhelmed. There were moments I questioned my sanity for staying. But somewhere along the way, something shifted. The small moments began to outweigh the grand gestures.

I remember graduation day vividly. Damon and I arrived early to secure seats as close to the stage as possible so I could take pictures. Tears welled up as I watched Bruno walk across that stage. After the ceremony, Damon and I hurried to find him amidst the families and friends taking photos. As we navigated the crowd, my phone rang. I felt a surge of excitement as I heard Bruno's voice describing his location; he stayed on the phone with me until we found him. When Damon asked why he hadn't called him, Bruno confidently replied, "Because I knew Stephanie would have her phone on her." In that moment, I wasn't invisible; I was chosen because I was trusted. That's the magic nobody tells you about: it's not about grand gestures or tearful heart-to-hearts; it's in those quiet moments when they choose you, when they trust you with what matters most.

Countless times, Bruno has asked me about important school

events. Even now, in college, he'll ask, "When is my spring break, winter break, and when does the semester start?" And guess what? I always know the answer. He knows he can rely on me. I was there helping and encouraging him when he got his first job at seventeen. He came to me to show and help him file his taxes, something we have done together for three years. But of all the times we shared, being the first person he reached out to on his high school graduation day, the first "parent" he hugged, that single moment was worth every sweat, tear, and laugh.

Then there's Rocco, my sweet, funny Rocco. We started watching shows together—not just kids' stuff, but movies and series I grew up with. He was genuinely excited to enjoy the things I loved. It sounds so simple, but it meant everything. He wasn't just tolerating his bonus mom's quirky taste in entertainment; he was choosing to share it with me.

Happy Bonus-Mom Day, Stephanie! I am so thankful for all the work you have put into me, always picking out fun activities for us to do while I'm down in Denver, and always getting excited to see me and look forward to spending time with me.
—Love, Rocco

One of the best days I ever had with Rocco was when we decided to hang out on the couch, wrapped in comfy blankets. We turned on a TV series we both wanted to watch and binged it all day. In between episodes, I made us breakfast and lunch, and we ate in front of the TV, continuing our marathon. No agenda. No trying to impress each other or prove anything. Just a bonus mom and her bonus kid, spending a day together doing nothing special, and it was everything.

That's when it hit me: this is it. This is what I was looking for. It wasn't some grand gesture or an Instagram-worthy moment. It was just us: comfortable, laughing, connecting, present, and real.

There have been moments of pure, magical connection with Damon, Bruno, and Rocco—times when we've laughed so hard we couldn't breathe, when we created memories that felt sacred. Seeing these boys grow into incredible young men, I've felt the deep, undeniable knowing that I played a part in that; that my love mattered, that my presence shaped who they are becoming.

But here's what I want you to know, because it's the most important thing: the blessing isn't that everything is perfect. The blessing is that I get to show up, even when it's messy and complicated and nothing like I imagined. The blessing is that I loved them through the hard parts, and they loved me back—not because they had to, but because we built something real together, and they chose to. The blessing is that I get to be seen by them, by my partner, and most importantly, by myself.

Stop waiting for validation from everyone else. Stop needing the biological mom to validate your role. Stop looking for permission to matter. You already do. You matter so much. Every time you showed up tired and still made dinner, every time you bit your tongue instead of saying what you really thought (that was extremely hard for me), every time you loved a kid who didn't ask for you—those moments are not ordinary; they are extraordinary.

You are not faint of heart. You walked into a terrifying situation and decided to love anyway. You had no roadmap, no guarantee of a happy ending, and you showed up with your whole heart anyway. That deserves endless celebration and recognition. You should look in the mirror and say, "I am a Badass Bonus Mom, and I earned this." Because you did. Absolutely.

Here's my advice, from one bonus mom to another: Be authentically you. The kids don't need perfect; they need real. They need to see you mess up and apologize. They need to know you're human. They need your vulnerability more than your perfection. Give yourself grace for the days you lose your patience, for the moments you feel resentful, for the times you wonder if you made the right choice.

Those moments don't make you a bad bonus mom; they make you human, and that's exactly who these kids need. With time, patience, and honest communication, you're building something that nobody can take away from you: a family. Your family. One that's uniquely yours, shaped by love and choice and the kind of commitment that doesn't come easy—which is exactly why it's so beautiful.

You deserve to feel like the luckiest woman in the world because you are. As you embrace this journey, remember that every moment—every laugh, every tear, and every day spent together—is a chance to weave your own magic. Celebrate the little victories that may seem small but hold immense significance.

Thanks, Michelle. I'm very grateful that you are in my life. Love you. —Bruno

Ladies, each step you take in this adventure is a testament to your strength, resilience, and capacity to love. You are not just a bonus mom; you are a vital thread in the tapestry of your family's story. The magic lies in your unwavering commitment, your ability to love without reservation, and your courage to navigate this beautifully complex journey.

Embrace the beautiful messiness of it all, knowing that you are exactly where you're meant to be. Your journey as a Badass

Bonus Mom is not just about the kids; it's about the extraordinary woman you are becoming. You are crafting a legacy filled with compassion, joy, and connection—one that will echo through the lives of those you love.

So, as you look ahead, remember: the magic of being a bonus mom isn't just in the moments shared; it's in the love you choose to give, the bonds you choose to nurture, and the family you continue to build. You are truly a force of nature, and your story is just beginning.

Embrace it all—unapologetically, fiercely, and with a heart full of love. The magic is yours to create, and there are countless adventures waiting to unfold.

The Beginning of Your Story

Over six years ago when I realized I wasn't going to be "the cool live-in girlfriend, I saw my life as chaotic—an obligation to be tolerated while waiting for my "real life" to begin. Now, surrounded by the sounds of a household brimming with unconditional love, I realize this is my real life, and I wouldn't trade it for anything.

As you close this book, remember that this is just the beginning of your own beautiful story. Every experience, challenge, and triumph is a chapter waiting to be written. Embrace your unique journey, knowing you are not alone.

Love should always take center stage. I haven't offered a roadmap to perfection because there is no such thing. Instead, I've shared the reality of this journey: the fights and breakthroughs, the doubt and the triumph. You are extraordinary not because you sacrifice yourself, but because you choose to be present in a messy, real life, building a family held together by love, not obligation.

When I met Damon, I thought I was gaining a partner, but

I gained a family. Two kids became integral to my life in unexpected ways, and I learned that the real challenge wasn't logistics, but trusting that I belonged. Remember, your worth, like mine, is never dependent on others' approval. If you're reading this, you are a woman who chose to love fiercely in a complex situation. You showed up, even when it was hard. You are a quiet warrior, building something beautiful every time you pack a lunch, attend a school play or sports activity, or support your partner. Your love proves that family isn't just about biology; it's about presence.

I've learned that you don't have to earn your place in this family. Belonging is something you claim by acting like you belong, setting boundaries to protect your peace, and speaking your truth—even when it's hard. Once you own your space, everything shifts. You become unmissable and essential.

As you return to your everyday life, remember that it will be both complicated and beautiful. Doubtful days will come, but know that you are exactly where you're meant to be—not because everything is perfect, but because you decided to be present regardless. You are choosing resilience and embracing the challenging work of building your unique family.

Remember, you don't have to do this alone. Seek out other women who understand this journey. Share your victories and struggles, lift each other up, and celebrate every success. Every woman who chooses to love fiercely within a blended family is part of a quiet revolution, and you are vital to it.

This book isn't a blueprint for perfection; it's a guide for the real journey. Use it as you need—read, reflect, and make it your own. Consider this a conversation between you and me, but more importantly, between you and yourself. The chaos, exhaustion, and doubt aren't signs of failure; they're signs that you're showing up authentically. That authenticity fosters connection and transforms a blended family into a true family.

Your bonus kids might not call you "mom," and they may test your patience, but they will also come to you with their heartbreak and dreams. They might light up when they see you and defend you to their friends and even their mom. That connection is the real reward.

Remember, you have the strength to navigate the complexities of blended families, the wisdom to learn from every moment, and the love to create lasting bonds. Let this book serve as a guide, a companion, and a source of inspiration as you write your own narrative filled with resilience, joy, and endless possibilities.

My final words: Own your space, set boundaries that protect your peace, speak your truth, and always remember that you are not a bonus. You're the architect of a new family. You are a Badass Bonus Mom who chose love over easy, and that choice is changing everything. Thank you for being part of this journey. Now, go live yours—unapologetically and fiercely. And who knows? This may just be the beginning of another badass bonus adventure together!

Xoxo,
Stephanie

Happy Badass Bonus Mom's Day

May feels different when you're a bonus mom. The world explodes with pastels, brunches, and handmade cards celebrating motherhood. Inevitably, there's that quiet moment—often in the grocery store checkout line, staring at the Mother's Day display—where you wonder, "Is this for me?" It's not about craving recognition or expecting a Hallmark moment; it's about the unique feeling of being celebrated as part of a family while simultaneously feeling excluded from the celebration itself. This feeling of invisibility is particular to bonus motherhood.

Over six years ago, I struggled to define my role. "Dad's girlfriend" felt temporary, like everything else in my life at that point. Then, five years ago, Bruno and Rocco helped me find the right word: "Bonus Mom." It wasn't loaded with fairy tales, nor was it about trying to be someone I wasn't; it was simply...ours.

Damon had a great idea: the weekend after Mother's Day would be dedicated to us—not as a replacement, but as an addition. A day where the boys could honor their mom, and then honor the relationship we had built together the following Sunday. It wasn't about competition, but about being seen. Damon continues to celebrate Bonus Mother's Day with me and the kids, a tradition he started when we first met, also honoring Mother's Day for my fur babies and the ones we share. Including his kids in the celebration signifies the value he places on me and our unique family dynamic.

And every year since, they've made sure I felt seen with cards containing handwritten messages and small gestures that conveyed, "We know what you do. We see you. You matter."

One card Bruno and Rocco purchased read:

Outside: **HAPPY MOTHER'S DAY! JUST THINK— THERE WAS ONCE A TIME WHEN YOU WEREN'T A MOTHER TO TWO OF THE GREATEST PEOPLE IN THE WORLD.**

Inside: **THANK GOODNESS WE CHANGED THAT, HUH? LOVE YOU!**

Messages the boys wrote inside:

Happy Mother's Day, Michelle. Thank you for always being there for me, even when I'm challenging.
Love you so much. —Love, Bruno.

Happy Bonus Mom Day, Stephanie! Thank you for being in our lives and picking out movies for me.
—Love, Rocco.

To every woman who fell in love with someone and, unexpectedly, gained a family: remember, you are not secondary, supplementary, or a supporting character in someone else's story. You are the woman who showed up when you didn't have to, who loved fiercely without any guarantee of reciprocation, and who navigated this role without a roadmap, job description, or even a universally agreed-upon title or marriage license. The moment you chose to stay, you took an unspoken oath: *I will love these children. I will honor their mother. I will build something real with this family.* And you have—every single day. Bravo!

So, if you haven't already, this month—and every month— know that YOU are vital and irreplaceable. You are exactly the person your family needed, even if it took them a while to realize it. You deserve to be celebrated, not as an afterthought or a bonus, but as the essential, powerful, badass woman you've always been.

Happy Badass Bonus Mom's Day!

Final Journal Prompt:

Reflect on Your Journey: Take a moment to explore your personal experience as a bonus mom. Consider these questions:

Take a moment to explore your personal experience as a bonus mom. Consider the following questions to guide your reflection:

- **What significant challenges have you faced, and how have they shaped you?**

Reflect on the obstacles that have tested your resilience and what you've learned from them.

- **Describe a moment when you felt truly connected to your bonus kids.**

What did that experience teach you about love, trust, and family?

- **How has your understanding of family evolved throughout this journey?**

Think about the transformations in your relationships and how they have deepened your sense of belonging.

- **How have you embraced the unknown, and how has it enriched your life?**

Consider the surprises and uncertainties you've encountered and the growth they've sparked within you.

- **What are your hopes and dreams for your family moving forward?**

Envision the future you aspire to create together and the legacy you wish to build.

Write freely and let your thoughts flow. There is no right or wrong way to express your feelings—this is your space to reflect, celebrate, and envision the future.

Happy Birthday Michelle!
I hope you have a great b-day with many more to come.
I appreciate all you have done for me thus far.
I know you will teach me many more lessons in the future,
Whether or not I like them in the moment,
I will understand + fully appreciate them later on.
I'm always eternally grateful for all
you have done + love that you are in my life.
Love, Bruno

Beyond Grateful

To everyone who purchased my book and joined me on this journey, thank you! Your belief in my story and support mean more than words can express. Together, we're building a community rooted in strength, resilience, and love. With each page, you demonstrate your commitment to growth and understanding in the world of bonus motherhood. I hope you find inspiration, empowerment, and connection within these pages, and that our shared journey continues to uplift and inspire us. Your support fuels my passion, and I am forever grateful to have you with me!

I want to express my heartfelt gratitude to Damon Miller, my favorite person, my partner, my love, and my best friend. Thank you for choosing me every day and for showering me with your unconditional love and support. I am deeply grateful for your trust in allowing me to be a part of your sons' lives; together, we've created a uniquely loving family. With you by my side, anything feels possible. Love you, bae.

To Bruno Miller, thank you for your big heart and the immense joy you bring into my life. Simply by being you, you remind me what it means to be truly incredible. Thank you for welcoming me into your life with open arms. I can't imagine a world without you as my bonus son; being your bonus mom is truly an honor. I love you so much!

Rocco, thank you for your quirky sense of humor and for allowing our relationship to grow at a pace that felt right for you. Watching you evolve has been a privilege, and your devotion and drive inspire me daily. Thank you for letting me be your bonus mom. I love you!

Kimberly Malone, thank you for being my best friend, my biggest cheerleader, and my spiritual sister throughout our friendship and this bonus mom journey. I couldn't have asked for a better support system. Laila, Ahmed, and Waleed are so lucky to have you as their bonus mom. Thank you, too, for the beautiful book cover! Inspired by you and your mom's spirit, you both created something truly magical that captures the essence of my book. I also appreciate the marketing mock-ups you made and your creative talents, but most of all, I appreciate you. I'm so grateful. Love you tons friend!

To my sister Tanya, thank you for always being there when I call and for being the steady voice I need. Since the moment I learned we were sisters, you've been my twin flame. Your presence strengthens my bonus mom journey in ways I can't fully express. Love you tons!

D'Vorah Bailey, thank you for your unwavering support and love—not just for me, but for my unique family. You always remind me of the strength we share when I need it most, and your advice has been invaluable. I'm grateful to have you as my sister, both growing up and now as adults. Love you, D!

Mom, Mary Roberts Bailey, thank you for all the laughter, your listening ear, and your steadfast support during my bonus mom journey. Your wise advice and encouragement mean everything to me. And thank you for raising me and being the mom God chose and I continue to choose daily. Love you, Mom!

Peggie Malone, thank you for the enduring inspiration you continue to bring to my life. Though you are with God, your spirit continues to encourage me. I am especially grateful for your role in my journey; you even inspired my book cover. Thank you for being the beautiful soul you were; your light shines brightly within us. Miss and love you!

Gwieneverea Brandon, thank you for being my best friend since we were five years old. Your unwavering support and kindness mean the world to me. I admire you not only as my friend, but also as one of the best mothers I know. You are not a bonus mom, however I've learned so much from your incredible parenting and the way you empower everyone around you. You inspire me every day! Love you!

Laura Di Franco, thank you for being an incredible inspiration. As a kick-ass mom navigating the world of publishing, your strength and passion uplift me every day. I am truly grateful to have you in my life. You embody what it means to pursue your dreams while nurturing your family, and your journey inspires me endlessly.

Kristin Kaplan, thank you for your kind and thoughtful review of my book. Thank you for being a positive light in my life, for your unconditional love, and for always being ready to chat about "kid talk." I cherish how our friendship continues to grow-you truly are one in a million! Love you!

Nancy Guin-DeBell, just hearing your voice brings calm to my spirit and joy to my heart. You infuse so much meaning into our friendship, and I feel incredibly blessed to have you in my life. Love you, Mama!

Krista Zizzo, thank you for being my rock throughout my bonus-mom journey. Your advice, listening ear, and unwavering support have been priceless. I appreciate you more than I can say. Love you!

To my four incredible bonus moms—Jean Koveos, the late Colleen Ennis (my biological Mom), the late Mrs. Gwieneverea Duncan, and the late Peggie Malone—thank you for the love and wisdom you have woven into my life. Each of you has played a vital role in shaping who I am today, and I am eternally grateful for your guidance and the unique gifts you brought into my life. Your legacies of love will forever live in my heart.

I want to express my sincere gratitude to Dusti Jones, Damon's incredible mother, for bringing such a remarkable man into the world. Damon has enriched my life immeasurably, blessing me with two amazing bonus sons and a vibrant, loving bonus family that I deeply cherish. Your warmth and kindness have made you a wonderful bonus mother-in-law, and I feel fortunate to have you in my life. You are an essential part of my journey, and I want you to know how much I love, respect, and appreciate you.

Paulette Henson, thank you for being a fierce inspiration in my life. You are also an incredible mother and a friend I am very proud and honored to have in my life. Love you.

Thank you to my friend, Deb DeVigne. From the moment I met Damon's boys, you opened your home and heart to me, creating a warm and welcoming environment that eased those initial moments. Thank you for sharing laughter and your friendship—it means the world to me. Love you.

Maggie McLaughlin, thank you for formatting another one of my books and for your meticulous attention to detail, ensuring my launch dates happen smoothly. I feel so lucky to have you on this journey with me.

Tara Backes, thank you for crafting my book marketing, managing my launch team, and creating my website. Your presence in my life makes everything less stressful, and I'm grateful for all you do!

About the Author

Stephanie is a clairvoyant, intuitive, and empathic life and love coach, mentor, and expert dedicated to empowering women to embrace their true potential in love and life. With over 26 years of experience coaching, guiding, and uplifting women, Stephanie brings heartfelt passion to every interaction. A Certified Master Life and Professional Coach and the CEO of Miss-Adventures, LLC, she is also a five-time #1 best-selling author, podcaster, and public speaker. Her writing has been featured in over 250 articles on platforms such as Hubpages, Paired Life, and Elephant Journal. Stephanie's diverse background includes over 17 years as a CorePower Yoga teacher and more than 25 years as an energy healer. She has shared her insights on numerous radio shows, podcasts, and women's panels. Stephanie believes that openness, honesty, and straightforwardness are crucial for achieving clarity and realizing one's aspirations. She passionately advocates for the transformative power of prayer and affirmations in manifesting love, health, wealth, success, family, abundance, fulfilling relationships, and overall prosperity. Stephanie's mission is to empower women on their life journeys, providing clear guidance in all matters of the heart. She offers both in-person and virtual coaching sessions to support you in pursuing your goals and dreams.

Connect with Stephanie:

- ★ Website: Miss-Adventures.com
- ★ Email: missadventureslovecoach@yahoo.com
- ★ Instagram: @miss_adventures_coach
- ★ Facebook: @missadventuresseries
- ★ LinkedIn: linkedin.com/in/miss-adventures
- ★ Scan the QR code for Life and Love Coaching sessions and packages.

Stephanie,

Some people enter our lives and quietly make everything better, wich is exactly what you've done for my boys. You chose to be a part of their lives, giving them something truly special. As they grow into young men, I see your influence in them, and I couldn't be more proud.

Thank you for your patience and encouragement, and for loving them simply because you wanted to. Being a bonus mom is one of the most underappreciated roles, but please know that your presence doesn't go unnoticed. You've made our family fuller and warmer, a gift I will never take for granted.

Love you so much, Princess,

Damon

Thank you, God, for the amazing people in my life—my family and friends—who have always been there for me. I'm also grateful for the guidance I've received while working on my new book, *Badass Bonus Moms: Strength, Love, and the Power of Showing Up.* I'm so happy to share the importance of being a bonus mom with all the women who have chosen this role, and I believe that with you, God, anything is possible!

Book cover illustrated by Peggie & Kimberly Malone
Book production and design by Second Star Publishing Works
Review inside book by Kristin Kaplan.
Mock-up book design for marketing by Kimberly Malone
Launch Team Executive by Tara Backer